WOODCARVING
WITH
RICK BÜTZ

WOODCARVING

WITH

RICK BÜTZ

By RICK and ELLEN BÜTZ

MADRIGAL

PUBLISHING COMPANY, INC.

Front cover photo by Anthony Tassarotti
Text photos by Ellen Bütz

Printed in the United States of America.

Third printing: August 1990

Library of Congress Cataloging-in-Publication Data:

Bütz, Richard.
   Woodcarving with Rick Bütz / by Rick and Ellen Bütz.
     p.   cm.
   ISBN 0-9617098-4-7 : $16.95
   1. Wood-carving—Patterns.   I. Bütz, Ellen   II. Title.
TT199.7.B89   1989
736'.4--dc19   88-39362
                                                CIP

Madrigal Publishing Company
517 Litchfield Road
P.O. Box 1629
New Milford, CT 06776

To Juliana, and her friends — the cats. For keeping life interesting.

This book and the television series it is based on would not have been possible without the help and cooperation of many people.

In particular we would like to thank all the woodcarvers across the country whose support and encouragement have meant so much to us.

Outstanding among them are our good friends, Bob and Anita Campbell, who have been a constant source of help, advice, and amusing stories.

A special thank you to our friends and woodcarving collectors, for their patience while we worked on these projects.

Our sincere thanks and appreciation to Sam Ross and the folks at Woodcraft for their major support in the production of the television series.

We would also like to thank all the folks at Madrigal Publishing, especially our editor, David Peters, for all their hours of hard work on this book.

And finally, a special thanks to Woodcarving's producer and director, Stephen Honeybill, and the rest of the team at WMHT-TV for giving us the opportunity to share our love of woodcarving with so many people.

Rick and Ellen Bütz
Blue Mountain Lake, New York
October, 1988

Table of Contents

Introduction

I guess it's no secret — I love woodcarving. For one thing, I love working with my hands, feeling a well-honed tool carve cleanly through the wood, and smelling the fragrant wood chips. I can just feel the tensions of daily life melt away.

Sometimes, when I'm really involved with a project, I almost feel like I'm in another time and place, a simpler world where the pace is set by the rhythm of tools carving through the wood, rather than by clocks or calendars. I always come back refreshed, with a new perspective on life.

Woodcarving has also given me a chance to meet a lot of new friends — especially through teaching. There's something exciting about introducing people to carving and watching them discover the rewards and satisfactions for themselves. That's why, when I was invited to help create a weekly public television series on woodcarving, I welcomed the opportunity to share my enjoyment with others.

Woodcarving is a simple art. You only need a few tools and basic techniques to get started; the rest comes with practice. But, once you have these basics, you're only limited by your imagination. You always have new horizons to explore. You can carve for a lifetime and never be bored.

With so many intriguing possibilities, it's a challenge to decide which carvings to include in a book like this. The following projects are some of my favorites. I hope you enjoy them too.

Happy carving,

Rick

Chapter 1

Tools
&
Sharpening

One of the best things about woodcarving is that you don't need many tools to begin. Figures like St. Nicklaus and the Doll Horse, and chip carvings such as the designs on the Salt Box and Quilt Rack projects can all be carved with a single knife. Although I've specified various carving tools for the projects, and they certainly add to the ease with which you can work, you can start carving right now using only a sharp pocket knife.

Before you begin though, there are several things that you need to know. The first and most important is how to sharpen your tools. There is a big difference between the drudgery of trying to force your way through a piece of wood with dull tools and the wonderful feeling of paring away clean shavings with sharp tools. You also need to develop a sensitivity to the nature of wood itself, a process carvers call "learning to work with the grain." In the following chapter we will cover both these subjects, so that when you tackle your first project you'll be able to experience all the joy woodcarving has to offer. ■

Tools & Sharpening

The beauty of woodcarving lies in its simplicity. All you really need to get started is a knife, a piece of wood, and a place to sit. This will provide you with all the necessary ingredients to create hundreds of different whittling and chip carving projects.

Later, when you feel ready to try your hand at making larger relief carvings and sculptures, you can begin adding some carving gouges to your tool collection. You only need a few to get started. On the Pineapple project for instance, I only used three gouges to create the whole carving. The point is that you don't have to rush out and accumulate a lot of tools right away — unless you want to.

At first glance, woodcarving gouges look a lot like chisels — except for one important difference — the blades are curved. This allows the tool to "scoop" out wood. Gouges are classified by the width of the blade (usually measured in millimeters) and the amount of blade curvature, which is called the "sweep." The sweep is usually indicated by numerals ranging from 1 to 11 stamped on the blade but some manufacturers have different numbering systems. The larger the number, the greater the curvature, and thus the larger the amount of wood the gouge will scoop out. The illustration shows 12 mm gouges. Notice how the curve changes as the number gets higher. There are also many other specialized gouges, including veiners, fishtail, macaroni, and spoon gouges. A quick look through a woodcarving supply catalog will show you the variety of tools that are available.

Photo 1

In addition to a knife and a few gouges, a mallet is also helpful on the larger carvings. The mallet is simply a round piece of heavy wood with a handle. It is used to tap the end of wide gouges to remove wood quickly. I prefer mallets made from lignum vitae. This dense tropical wood has interlocking fibers that resist splitting (Photo 1).

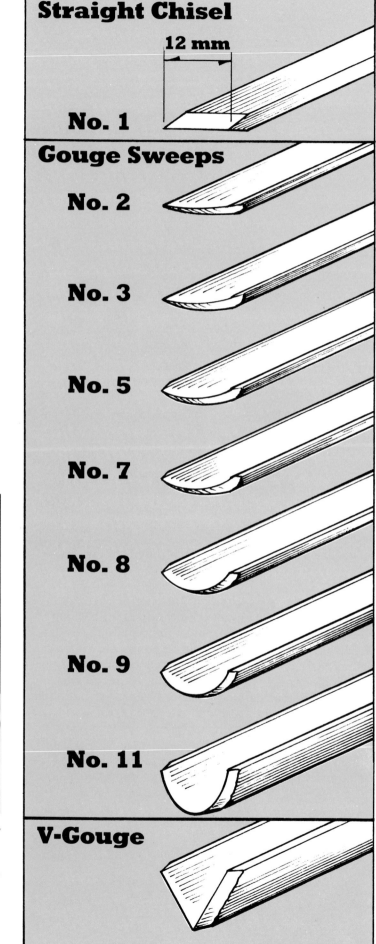

Straight Chisel

12 mm

No. 1

Gouge Sweeps

No. 2

No. 3

No. 5

No. 7

No. 8

No. 9

No. 11

V-Gouge

Tools & Sharpening

However, even the best quality carving tools won't produce good carvings unless they are properly sharpened. The crisp, clean tool marks left by a well-honed knife or gouge are the sign of a serious craftsman. Besides, a sharp tool is actually safer to use than a dull one. It requires less force to move through the wood, making it easier to control, with less chance of slipping. And carving is a lot more fun when the tools glide easily through the wood, making smooth, polished cuts.

There are as many different ways to sharpen tools as there are woodcarvers. This can be a bit confusing to newcomers. The method that works best for me begins with a medium/fine oil stone. The one I use is called an India Stone. This stone has a fine side and a medium side, and can be found in just about any hardware store. Always use oil with this type of stone. It lubricates the tool on the stone, and floats away any tiny bits of metal that would otherwise clog the stone and lessen its cutting power.

Photo 3

After a minute or so, turn the blade over and sharpen the other side the same way. As the abrasive stone wears away the steel, a thin metal foil will form along the cutting edge of the knife. This is called the burr, or wire edge. It is so small that you can't see it without a magnifying glass. Check for it by lightly dragging your fingertip across the knife blade away from the cutting edge (Photo 3).

Photo 2

To sharpen your knife, first put several drops of light household oil (sewing machine oil) on the fine side of the sharpening stone. Place your knife on the stone at a 25-degree angle and move it back and forth along the length of the stone. Use medium pressure — about as hard as you would press down when writing with a ball-point pen (Photo 2).

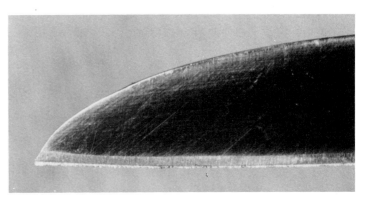

Photo 4A

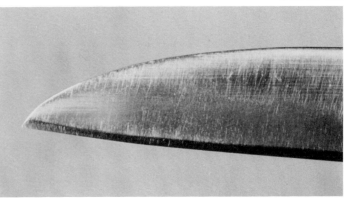

Photo 4B

Check both sides of the blade. The burr will feel like a thin, rough edge of metal that catches on the ridges of your fingertips. Continue sharpening until you can feel the burr along the entire edge of the blade (Photo 4A). When you reach this point, the knife is as sharp as it will get on the stone. However, don't try carving with it yet, because the burr will either bend over or break off, leaving you with a dull knife.

Tools & Sharpening

Photo 5

When you are through stropping, test the edge of your blade for sharpness. Take a piece of soft wood like white pine or basswood and make a test cut across the end grain, which is the edge of the wood where you can see the annual growth rings (Photo 6). If the knife is razor sharp, it will remove a clean chip with a slight whistling sound. However, if the wood crunches and tears, the blade needs more stropping.

To remove the burr, use a strop. This is simply a strip of leather tacked down to a piece of wood. The leather serves as a very fine sharpening stone.

To strop the knife, hold it at a 25-degree angle to the strop and stroke the blade along the leather in a direction away from the cutting edge (Photo 5). To make the strop work more quickly, you can rub a little fine abrasive like jeweler's rouge into the leather.

Stroke the knife along the leather 10 times on one side, lift the blade completely off the leather, turn it over, and strop the other side 10 times. Repeat this procedure until you can no longer feel a burr. You may find this will take 15 to 30 minutes (Photo 4B).

Photo 7

Use the same basic procedure to sharpen a gouge. The main difference is in the motion you use for sharpening the cutting edge on the stone. For the gouge, the tool is placed at about a 30-degree angle to the stone. Rub it along the length of the stone, rotating the tool as you go, so the entire cutting edge gets sharpened (Photo 7). When you can feel the burr on the gouge, put the sharpening stone away.

You can use the leather strop to remove the burr. However, the curved shape of the cutting edge does take longer to polish than the flat blade of a knife. A quicker way to do this is to use a slip stone. This is a small abrasive stone with one rounded edge and one sharply angled edge. My favorite slip stone, called a fine white Arkansas, is made from a natural rock mined for its excellent abrasive qualities.

Photo 6

Photo 8

Holding the slip stone in your right hand, place a few drops of oil on the stone's rounded edge. Then, take the gouge in your left hand and rub the slip stone briskly along the inside diameter, which is the cutting edge of the blade (Photo 8). Continue until you can no longer feel the burr.

Photo 10

Photo 9

For a final touch, you can polish the bevel of the gouge on the strop. The tool will guide more smoothly through the wood if the bevel is polished. Stroke the blade gently along the length of the leather away from the cutting edge. This will remove any microscopic remnants of the burr edge, and polish away any scratches left by the sharpening stone.

Test the sharpness of your gouge by making a practice cut across the grain on a piece of pine or basswood. If your gouge is dull it will crush and tear the wood fibers (Photo 9). But, if it is sharp it will make a clean cut (Photo 10).

Photo 11

All gouges are sharpened basically the same way regardless of the sweep. The only exception is the V-gouge (also sometimes called parting tool). This extremely useful tool is one of the trickiest to sharpen properly.

Begin by treating each side of the V-gouge as a tiny knife, and sharpen it by sliding it back and forth on the stone (Photo 11). Each side of the V-gouge is held at a

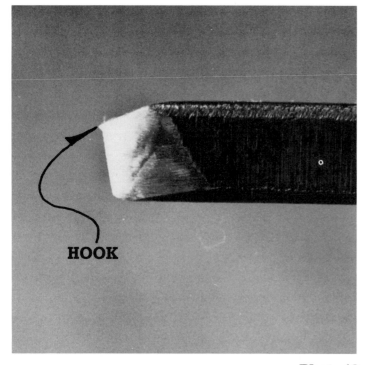

HOOK

Photo 12

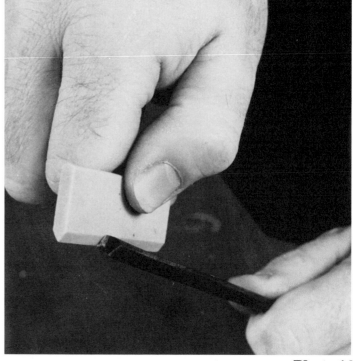

Photo 14

Photo 13

Photo 15

25-degree angle to the sharpening stone, just as the knife was. This sharpening motion will hone the flat sides of the gouge, but the V-profile of the cutting edge will cause a small "hook" to form at the point of the V (Photo 12). You have to remove the hook before the tool will cut properly. Otherwise, it will plow into the wood and cause splinters. Remove the hook by treating the bottom of the V like a miniature gouge. Gently rock it back and forth on the stone with the same motion used on the other carving gouges (Photo 13).

Use the angled edge of the slip stone to remove the burr on the inside bevel (Photo 14). Polish the outer bevel with the leather strop. When your V-gouge is properly sharpened it will look like this (Photo 15).

Tools & Sharpening

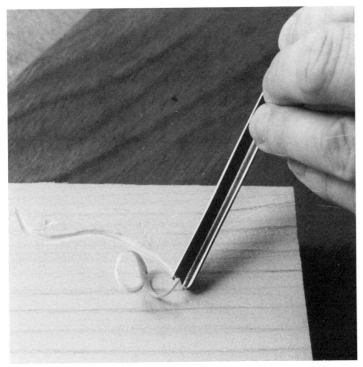

Photo 16

Check the sharpness of your V-gouge by cutting cross-grain on a piece of soft wood (Photo 16). It should cut smoothly and cleanly without tearing the wood.

After your tools are sharp, you are ready to begin carving. However, even with perfectly honed tools, you still need to give some consideration to your wood.

Just about all of the projects that follow are carved from either basswood or white pine. These woods can be purchased at lumber stores or woodworking supply companies. You can also use other woods for carving, but for the projects in this book the wood should be soft and have an even grain.

Photo 18

Grain simply means the texture of the wood. Each type of wood is made up of microscopic hollow wood fibers. They give each species its individual characteristics such as density, color and hardness.

The arrangement of fibers also determines how you shape the wood. The carving tool must be worked in the same direction that the wood fibers overlay each other. This is called "carving with the grain." For example, even with a sharp tool it is possible to create rough splinters when carving if the tool is cutting against the alignment of the fibers (Photo 17). Instead, if you cut from the opposite direction into the wood, the same cutting edge will produce nice clean shavings (Photo 18).

Carving with the grain is mostly a matter of developing a feel for it, even an ear for it. Carving against the grain makes a distinctive crunching sound. Carving with the grain makes a soft whistling sound.

Don't worry about trying to figure this out with logic. In time you will develop an instinct for the correct direction. It's a lot like petting a dog or a cat. One way feels right, and the other direction feels rough (to you and your pet).

So get your carving tools sharpened up and get ready to start your favorite project. ■

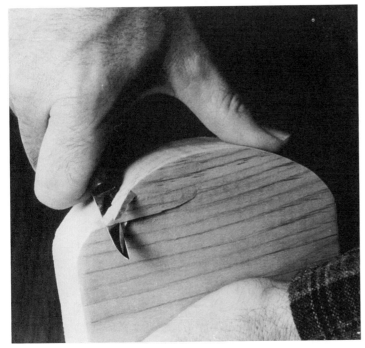

Photo 17

Chapter 2

Whittling

To me, whittling is making a carving small enough to hold in your hands and shape with a few simple tools. You only need a knife and perhaps one or two small gouges to create a variety of different woodcarvings. Whittling is the oldest style of woodcarving and began when early man discovered he could shape pieces of wood with a sharp stone.

Centuries later, when people discovered how to forge metal tools, whittling became more sophisticated. During long evenings around the fireplace, country folks carved items they needed for everyday life and decorated them with simple designs. In time, whittling pieces just for fun became a cultural tradition, and each different region developed its own distinctive style.

The projects in this chapter are some of my favorites from around the world. Each one is rooted in the heritage of the region it springs from. These carvings have long given joy and pleasure, both to the carver as he makes them and to family and friends who receive them as gifts.

As you are carving, always remember to work at a comfortable pace, and enjoy the feeling that you are helping to continue a centuries-old tradition. I've really had fun making these woodcarvings and hope you will too. ■

Swedish Folk-Art Doll Horse

Color Photo Page 41

Swedish Folk-Art Doll Horse

This folk toy, called a Dalahast, originated in the Dalerna province of Sweden. Its name means simply "horse from Dala."

The farming folk of this province have long been known for their colorful paintings and carvings. The tradition is believed to have started years ago during the long winter evenings when fathers would sit around the blazing hearth, talking and telling stories — and carving the little wooden figures for their children.

Eventually this became a productive cottage industry, and the men of Dala would set out each spring with wagon loads of toys and other homemade articles to barter for grain. Along the way, the little painted horses would often be given to a farmer's children in appreciation for a night's lodging.

Today the Dalahast are carved mainly by two families in Nissergarden in the Mora region of central Sweden. They are usually dark blue or reddish orange with painted decorations for the harness and saddle. This style of Swedish painting is called "krusning" and is similar to Norwegian "rosemaling."

Traditionally these horses were whittled from white pine or spruce in a variety of sizes from 1½ in. to several inches in height. Feel welcome to vary the size if you like. No matter what the size, the carving procedure is exactly the same.

I made this carving from a block of air-dried white pine, about 1¾ in. thick by 4½ in. square. I recommend that you use air-dried pine if you can find it, since it's much softer and less brittle than pine that has been kiln dried. Basswood would also be a good choice.

Swedish Folk-Art Doll Horse

Photo 1

Begin by tracing the full-size horse pattern on a piece of thin paper. Typing paper works fine. Cut the pattern out and position it on your block of wood. Make sure the grain direction is running the length of the legs for maximum strength. Then, just draw around the outline to transfer the pattern to the wood (Photo 1).

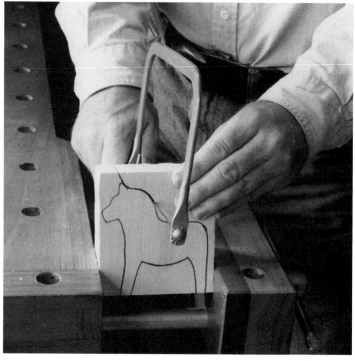

Photo 2

Cut out the horse with a coping saw (Photo 2). On a country-style carving like this, it seems natural to use traditional hand tools. You could also use a band saw if you have one.

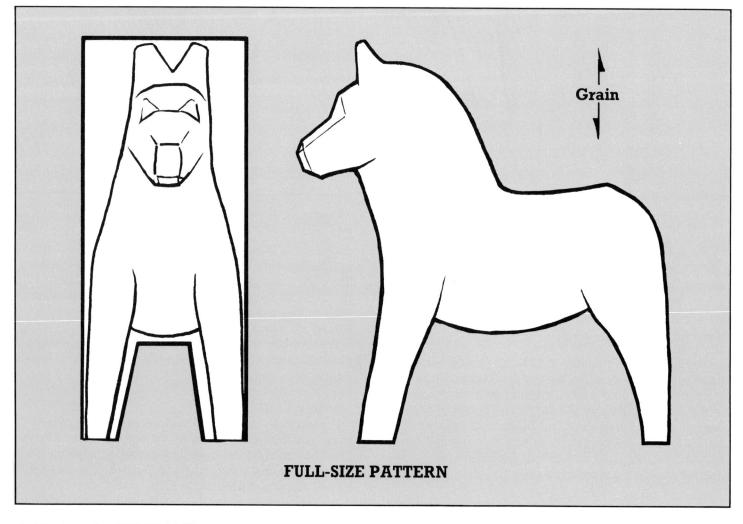

Grain

FULL-SIZE PATTERN

Swedish Folk-Art Doll Horse

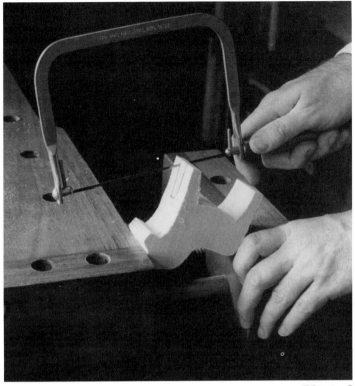

Photo 3

Next, use the coping saw to cut out a section ½ in. wide and 1½ in. deep between the front legs (Photo 3). (Don't try this with a band saw; it isn't safe.) Do the same for the hind legs. When using the coping saw, go gently, because the blade is very thin and can break easily. Let the saw do the cutting; don't force it.

Photo 5

For a traditional whittling project like this one, I use two basic knife cuts: the paring cut and the levering cut. For the paring cut (Photo 5), place your thumb on the block of wood and slowly close your hand as you draw the knife through the wood. Keep your thumb low enough on the piece of wood so the knife doesn't hit it.

You can use this paring cut to do most of the shaping on the horse. Start by simply rounding off all the corners on the body.

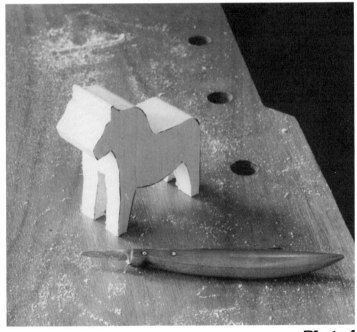

Photo 4

When the blank is completely cut out it will look like this (Photo 4). I use a small German carving knife to shape the horse. You can also use a pocket knife, but I find the large wooden handle of the carving knife smoother and more comfortable to hold.

Photo 6

The levering cut (Photo 6) is handy for getting into areas that are hard to reach with the paring cut. Place your left thumb on the back of the knife blade and pivot the knife, using your thumb as a fulcrum. This allows you to nibble off small chips of wood very precisely.

Swedish Folk-Art Doll Horse

Remember, these are small controlled movements using only the muscles of your fingers and hand. It's dangerous to pull a knife through wood toward you with the full power of your arm. Whenever I start feeling impatient, I think of the old woodcarvers' saying, "Three small chips are better than one big one."

Photo 9

Photo 7

The next step is to thin down the neck and head. Carve away wood from each side until the horse is about ¾ in. thick at the ears (Photo 7).

Photo 10

Your horse should be nicely rounded all over. Smooth off the square edges of the head, and for the finishing touch, cut a notch between the ears (Photo 10).

You can use a little fine sandpaper to smooth off areas between the legs and under the chin where it's difficult to get a clean cut. I prefer 220-grit garnet or aluminum oxide paper because it lasts longer than the inexpensive flint paper. Don't sand off all the tool marks, though. They give the doll horse his charming folk-art look.

Photo 8

To create the separation of the legs and body, first use the levering cut to round off the stomach of the horse (Photo 8). Then make a shallow vertical cut pressing the knife down to cut the chip free (Photo 9).

Use this same technique on all four legs; then round and taper the legs slightly.

Swedish Folk-Art Doll Horse

Photo 11

These horses were traditionally painted dark blue or orange. To seal the wood and create a smoother painting surface, I recommend brushing or spraying a light coat of lacquer on the horse before you paint. This isn't essential, but it does make painting easier.

On this project, I used enamels for their bright, cheerful colors and quick drying time. Model-painting enamels such as Testor's are available at hobby and art supply stores. First paint on a base coat of blue with a soft, flat brush (Photo 11). I used a no. 8 brush with synthetic sable bristles.

Photo 12

Let your horse dry thoroughly. Then paint on his festive harness with the same type of enamel. A small pointed no. 2 sable brush works well for the fine lines (Photo 12). Use a no. 4 flat sable brush with the larger areas like the saddle blanket.

Don't worry about making him perfect. The originals are painted in a free, casual style. In folk art a few slips just add to the authenticity.

The doll horse is really fun to carve and paint, and it makes a great gift for both children and adults. I enjoy making each new one more than the one before, and I use a slightly different color scheme and pattern so each horse is unique. Once your family sees this little fellow, you'll probably end up making several of these delightfully easy-to-make folk carvings. ■

Russian Dancing Bears

Color Photo Page 42

Russian Dancing Bears

nother region that produces distinctive folk toys is Eastern Europe, particularly Russia. These Dancing Bears are a traditional favorite. We patterned our bears after toys from the village of Bogorodsk near Moscow. For centuries this area has been famous for woodcarving, especially carved toys. It's a cottage industry, with the whole family helping out, using only simple tools such as a knife, drill and a few gouges.

There is a lot of satisfaction in recreating these traditional folk toys. I like the feeling you get of touching the past as you carve away the chips, just as the European folk carvers did. And you also end up with a toy that has an amusing charm all its own.

These dancing bears have always been one of my favorites. As the wooden ball swings around in a circle below the toy, it pulls the strings in sequence to create the action. One bear beats on the drum with a steady tippity-tap while the other bear stomps his foot up and down keeping time. The bears seem to bring out a smile in everyone who sees them.

The paddle for this carving can be made from just about any wood that you have on hand. You'll need a piece about 5 in. by 7 in. and ½ in. to ¾ in. thick. I used cherry because of its pretty grain and warm color, and I just happened to have a piece the right size in my workshop. For the bears, however, a soft wood is best.

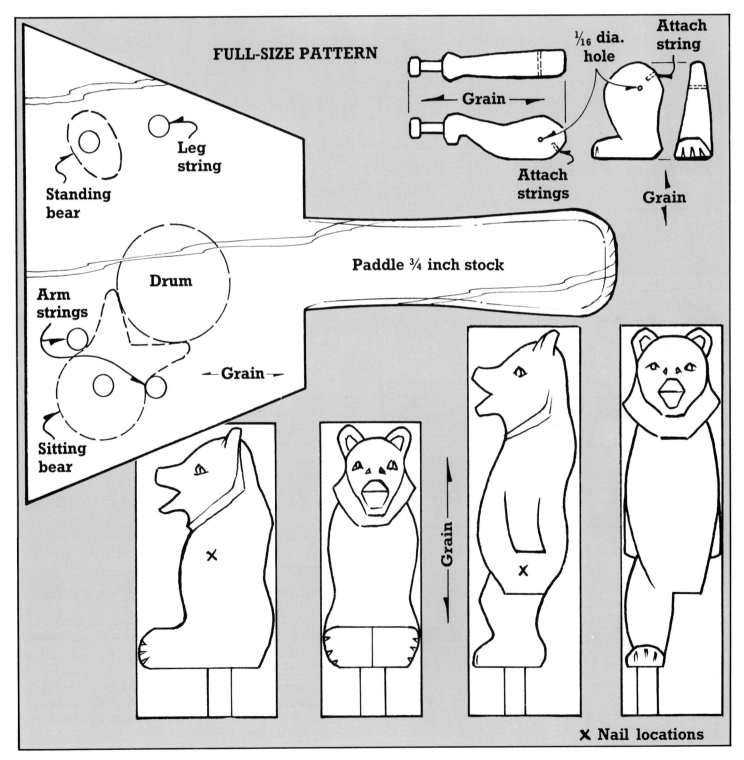

FULL-SIZE PATTERN

¹⁄₁₆ dia. hole

Attach string

Grain

Standing bear

Leg string

Attach strings

Grain

Drum

Paddle ¾ inch stock

Arm strings

Grain

Sitting bear

Grain

✕ Nail locations

Russian Dancing Bears

Air-dried white pine or basswood would be fine. The original Russian toys appear to be made from a European aspen. The bears are so small that a piece 6 in. square and 1½ in. thick is enough for all the parts, including the drum and the ball.

Photo 1

Trace the side profiles of the two bears, the arms, and the leg parts onto the stock, using the full-size patterns. Also lay out the profile of the ¾ in. thick drum, and a 1¼ in. diameter blank for the ball. Then cut all the pieces out with a coping saw. You may use a band saw if you have one (Photo 1), but be sure to wear eye protection and roll up your sleeves to avoid getting them caught in the machinery. Note that you only need to cut out the side view of the bears, since the rest is shaped with carving tools.

Photo 2

When you have all the pieces cut out they will look like this (Photo 2).

Photo 3

Begin rounding the handle on the paddle so that it fits comfortably in your hand (Photo 3). The rest of the paddle is traditionally left plain. Use 220-grit sandpaper to smooth off any rough edges.

Photo 4

Draw the pattern for the front view of the bears on the backs of the blanks you cut out. Then start rounding out the standing bear with your whittling knife (Photo 4). Just carve away the sharp corners. Don't worry about detailing the body at this point; we'll use a gouge to texture the fur later.

Russian Dancing Bears

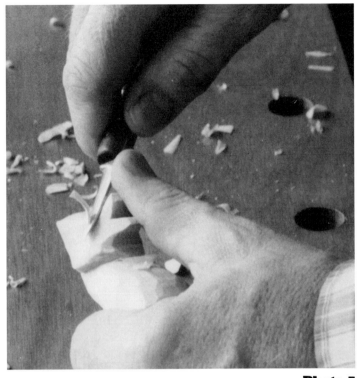

Photo 5

Carve the face by rounding off the general shapes, and then narrow the muzzle (Photo 5). Make two tiny chips on each side of the nose to shape the nostrils.

Photo 6

The eyes are a bit trickier. First, draw out the location with a pencil. Next, holding the knife in a pencil grip, incise a shallow (1/16 in. or less) vertical cut along your pencil lines (Photo 6). For the pencil grip, simply hold the knife as you would a pen or a pencil. With your middle finger braced against the flat side of the blade near the point, slowly make a cut just as you would

Photo 7

draw a line with a pencil. For added control you can actually brace your little finger right on the wood. Make sure your knife is razor sharp so your cuts will be clean and crisp. Whittle out the tiny triangular chips on either side of the eye (Photo 7), and round the pupil by beveling the sharp edges very slightly.

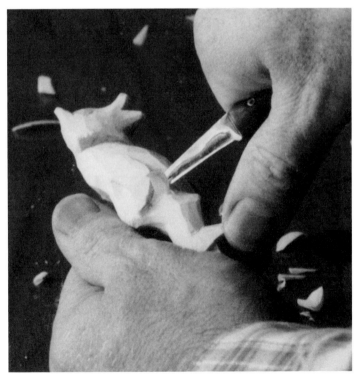

Photo 8

To shape the arm on the standing bear, incise a line about 1/8 in. deep around the outline using your knife in the pencil grip. Then pare away the wood around the arm so that it is left raised above the body (Photo 8).

Russian Dancing Bears

Use a 7 mm no. 8 gouge to texture the fur. Make short cuts to suggest a bear's shaggy coat (Photo 9). Use the pencil grip and gently push the gouge through the wood with your fingertips. Don't push with your whole arm, because it's too difficult to control. You might take off more wood than you want. Remember, don't let the fingers of your left hand get in front of the cutting edge of the gouge.

For the final step in the bear's body, whittle the tenon, or peg, on the bottom of his foot. Make it ¼ in. diameter.

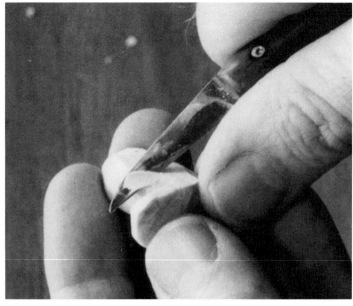

Photo 10

Now, you're ready for the leg. Drill a tiny $\frac{1}{16}$ in. hole through the top of the leg before you begin carving it. The hole will keep the leg from splitting when you tack it to the body, and also allow it to pivot freely so your bear can dance.

Start carving the leg by tapering it so that the top end is about ⅛ in. thick and the foot end is ⅜ in. thick. Then just round off the angles (Photo 10).

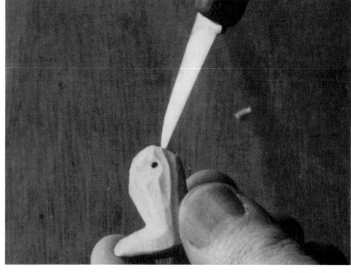

Photo 11

To make the foot move up and down, you need to fasten a piece of string about 12 in. long to the back of the leg. Later on this string will be fastened to the weight that hangs below the paddle. I used a kite string, but any fine cotton or synthetic string will do. With the point of your knife, make a small hole in the leg, referring to the pattern for the location. Twist the knife tip back and forth a little to drill the hole ⅛ in. deep or less (Photo 11).

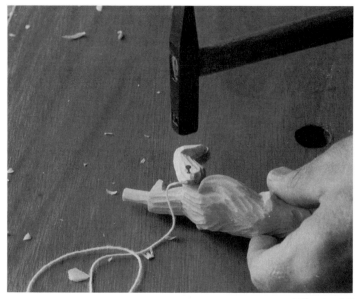

Photo 12

Place a small drop of wood glue, like Titebond, on the end of a toothpick and work it into the hole. Let it dry for one or two minutes until it becomes tacky. Then press the end of the string into the glue with a toothpick. Let the glue dry completely.

When the glue is dry, tack the leg to the body with a ½ in. by no. 18 wire nail. Start the hole in the body with a scratch awl or large needle so the nail will go in more easily. Use a small tack hammer and tap gently to avoid splitting the wood (Photo 12).

Use the same technique to carve the sitting bear and to attach his arms. Make the arms ¼ in. thick.

Russian Dancing Bears

Photo 13

While you're waiting for the glue to dry between the various steps, whittle a round ball about 1¼ in. diameter (Photo 13). This is the weight that powers the movement of the dancing bears.

Photo 14

After the bears are completed, with their strings glued in place, you're ready to assemble the toy.

Drill ¼ in. holes in the paddle in the locations marked on the full-size pattern. Position the bears in the holes and glue the drum into position. Make sure the bear's arms hit the drum surface. If the bears are loose in their holes, you can glue them in. On the original Russian toy, the bears fit snugly enough that glue wasn't necessary (Photo 14).

Photo 15

Holding the paddle up, gather the three strings together and tie them in a knot about 5 in. below the center of the paddle. To attach the weight, tie another knot about 1 in. below the first around a no. 18 wire nail. Tack this nail with the knot tied around it into the weight. Trim off the excess string ends with a pair of scissors (Photo 15).

Traditionally, a toy like this is left unfinished, although you could apply a coat of clear Minwax or other penetrating oil finish if you wanted it sealed for protection against dust and moisture. A word of caution: Small parts present a choking hazard, so small children shouldn't play with this toy.

Even though this is called a toy, I find adults get as much enjoyment out of it as children, and it's sure to delight both young and old for years to come. ■

St. Nicklaus

Color Photo Page 42

St. Nicklaus

Many of our Christmas customs come from Germany, among them the Christmas tree and several favorite carols. None, though, has found a warmer place in our hearts than St. Nicklaus.

The roots of the St. Nicklaus tradition go back several centuries to a certain early bishop who, because of his legendary acts of kindness, became the patron saint of students and children. In time, St. Nicklaus' feast day, December 6, was celebrated by the giving of gifts to small children in the saint's name.

As the tradition flourished in the remote Black Forest region of Germany, small figures of St. Nicklaus, like this one, were often whittled as gifts. These early carvings were usually blue or green or even brown, instead of the red we've come to associate with "Santa Claus."

I love to make these little carvings in the fall when the chill in the air reminds me that winter isn't far away. It seems that some of the magic of Christmas is reflected in the feeling that I always get when suddenly, after hours of patient whittling on a block of wood, a little person appears to be looking back at me. The carving really seems to take on a life of its own.

Try carving St. Nicklaus and I think you'll feel the magic yourself.

I used air-dried white pine for this St. Nicklaus. Pine is a traditional carving wood in the mountain regions where this type of figure was first carved. I love the fragrant scent of the pine shavings, reminding me of Christmas trees and pine bough decorations.

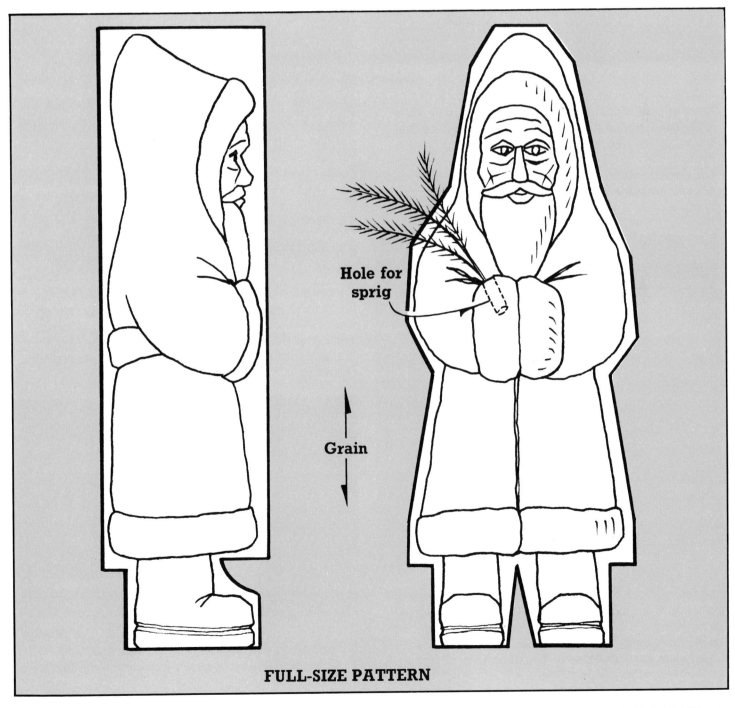

Hole for sprig

Grain

FULL-SIZE PATTERN

St. Nicklaus

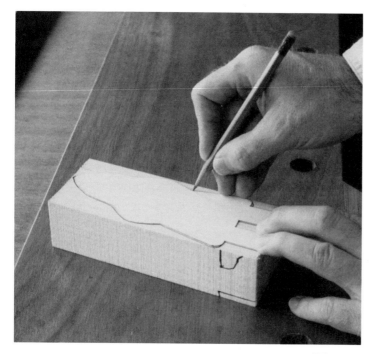

Photo 1

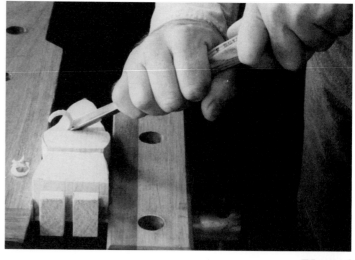

Photo 3

Begin by drawing the front and side views of St. Nicklaus on a block of wood 2½ in. by 6½ in. by 1¾ in. thick. You'll notice that I only drew in the feet on the side view; the rest will be shaped with carving tools (Photo 1). Cut out the blank on a band saw beginning with the side view. This will leave you with a flat surface to rest your blank on when cutting out the front view (Photo 2).

Photo 4

Fasten the carving in the vise and use a V-gouge, 6 mm to 10 mm wide, to mark the top and bottom of his sleeves (Photo 3). Then use a flat 30 mm no. 2 gouge and bevel the wood down to the level of the V-gouge cut on either side of the sleeves, leaving them raised (Photo 4).

Photo 2

If you have a carving bench with a vise and some gouges, you can begin this carving in the same way a mountain woodcarver of a small Alpine village would. In roughing out, the gouges are more efficient than a knife, since they take off the waste wood more quickly. Otherwise, you can carve St. Nicklaus entirely with a knife, but it takes a little longer.

Photo 5

Turn the carving sideways in the vise and use a V-gouge to make a diagonal cut to outline the bottom of the arm (Photo 5).

St. Nicklaus

Photo 6

Then round off the sharp corners of the block with the no. 2 gouge (Photo 6). Continue rounding over to the middle of the back. Do the same on the other side, using the V-gouge to outline the arm, and the flat gouge to round the corners. The back should be slightly rounded.

Photo 7

Now that most of the excess wood has been removed, take the carving out of the vise. The rest of the work on St. Nicklaus will be done while he's held in your hand.

Use the V-gouge again to outline the belt with a shallow cut. Hold the gouge the way you would hold a pencil and gently push it through the wood with your fingertips. Remember, don't let the fingers of your left hand get in front of the cutting edge of the gouge (Photo 7). Notice that I've wrapped heavy string around part of the shaft of the blade. The string makes the tool more comfortable to hold when you're making this type of cut. I learned this technique while visiting some woodcarvers in Switzerland. It really helps.

Photo 8

Now use your carving knife to pare the wood on either side of the belt down to the cut. This leaves the belt raised above the cloak (Photo 8).

Use the same techniques to make a ½ in. wide ruff around the hem of St. Nicklaus' cloak.

Photo 9

Next, shape the feet by rounding off the sharp angles (Photo 9). Be careful not to carve against the grain. You can tell when this is happening because your knife starts digging into the wood, making splinters. If that happens, reposition your hands and the wood so you're carving from the opposite direction.

Working with the grain is especially important around the feet because the toes are fragile. Carving against the grain can easily split them off. If a toe does break off, glue it back in place with some wood glue and continue carving when it has dried.

Photo 10

After shaping the boot, use the V-gouge to incise a very shallow line around the bottom to form the sole of the boot (Photo 10).

Photo 12

With your knife, round the back of the head to form St. Nicklaus' hood. Then carve the top of the hood down so it slopes toward the face (Photo 12).

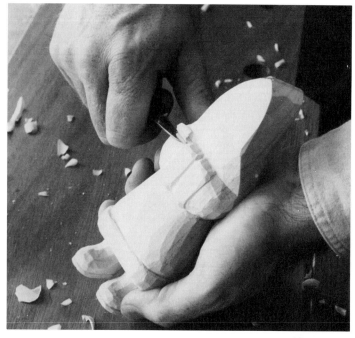

Photo 11

Next, mark out the cuffs on the sleeves by making a shallow cut down the center of the sleeve area, and a cut about ½ in. on either side of it with the V-gouge. Then pare away the wood of the sleeves leaving the cuffs raised (Photo 11).

Photo 13

Draw a line around the hood about ¼ in. back from the face. Then cut along it with your V-gouge (Photo 13).

St. Nicklaus

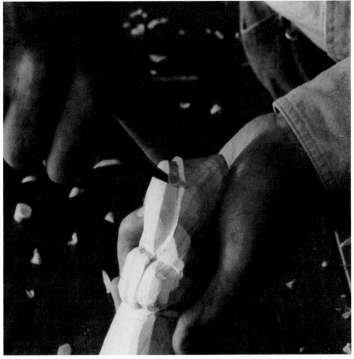

Photo 14

Next, use your knife to pare away the excess on the face side of your V-gouge cut (Photo 14). Repeat this procedure until the face is about ⅞ in. wide with ¼ in. of hood standing proud around it.

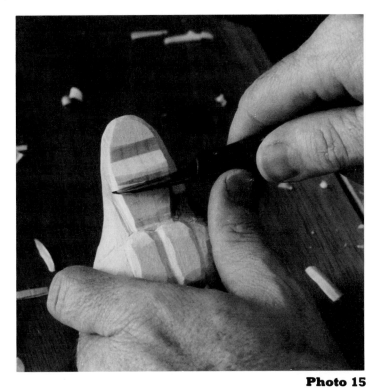

Photo 15

Draw a line for the eyes ½ in. down from the top of the forehead, and draw another line ½ in. below that for the bottom of the nose. Then make two notches about ⅛ in. deep where you drew the lines (Photo 15).

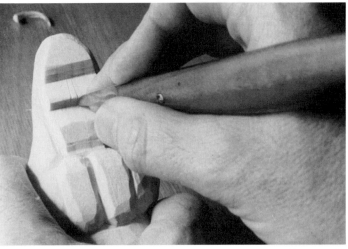

Photo 16

The next several steps of carving the face can be a bit tricky. You may want to practice on a scrap of wood to get a feeling for carving the details.

Holding the knife in the pencil grip, incise the two lines that will form the sides of the nose (Photo 16). Then

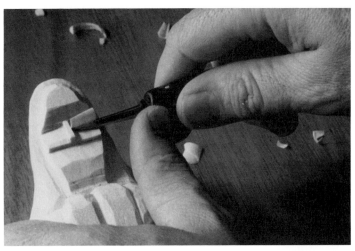

Photo 17

pare away the excess wood over the cheeks (Photo 17). To shape the cheek, remove a small triangular chip by making a vertical cut between the cheek and the nose and then making a small horizontal cut to slice the chip free (Photo 18). Then round over the sharp angles on the cheek and forehead.

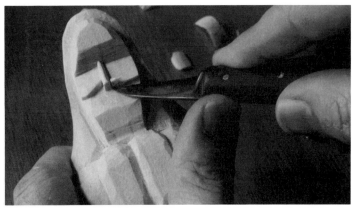

Photo 18

St. Nicklaus

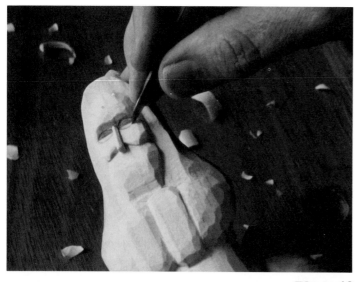

Photo 19

Photo 20

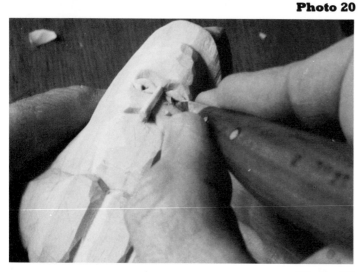

Photo 21

triangular chip of wood from the bottom eyelid by taking the point of your knife and making three cuts angled so they meet at the bottom (Photo 21). At this point, you'll really start to see St. Nicklaus in the wood.

Photo 22

Next, holding the knife in the pencil grip, draw a line to establish the lower edge of the mustache and a second line for the lower edge of the mouth (Photo 22).

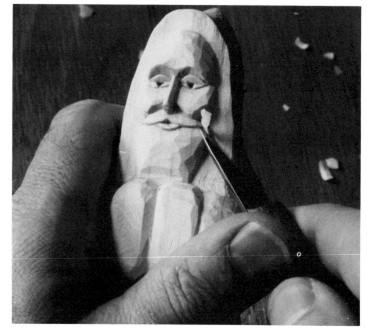

Photo 23

Then use the point of the knife and pare away a thin chip below each of the cuts (Photo 23). This is similar to the technique used to shape the eye.

To shape the eyes, hold the knife in the pencil grip and incise a very shallow cut (about $\frac{1}{32}$ in. deep) around the outline of the eye (Photo 19). Then carefully slice away a very thin chip above and below the eye area (Photo 20). To make the pupil of the eye, remove a tiny

St. Nicklaus

Photo 24

Now that the face is done, you're ready to start the finishing details. Use a V-gouge to texture the long hair of the beard and mustache. A little 3 mm V-gouge is perfect for this if you have one (Photo 24).

Photo 25

With the V-gouge, carve a line around the hood meeting at the beard to form the fur ruff on the hood. Round it slightly with a knife.

Then, using the V-gouge again, make a series of short cuts to create the fur texture on the cuffs, hem, and hood of St. Nicklaus' cloak (Photo 25).

The carving is now done. But before you start painting, drill a small hole at a downward angle in the crook of his arm. This will hold the traditional good luck sprig from your Christmas tree.

Photo 26

The painting techniques used on this carving are very simple. For St. Nicklaus' white beard and eyebrows and the trim on his cloak, use white acrylic paint thinned with water to a good brushing consistency. For these areas, I find acrylic covers better than oil paint. But for the other colors, I use oils since they have a softer look.

After the white paint has dried, you may paint the cloak any color you choose. I like cerulean blue, because it is very close to the azure color traditionally used in some areas of Germany.

Squeeze a little oil paint into a saucer and thin it with turpentine until it becomes a transparent stain. This paint mixture will allow the wood grain to show through and add extra character to your carving. Paint it on the carving with a soft sable brush (Photo 26). Paint the boots and belt with black oil paint also thinned to a stain with turpentine. As a historical note, this style of painting is called tinting and is seen on many of the old European woodcarvings.

You may find yourself carving several of these for friends and family. Although some of the fine details may be challenging, this type of woodcarving gets easier to do with each new one you make. ■

Alvah Dunning & Hound

Color Photo Page 43

Alvah Dunning & Hound

Here in the United States we have regions with a heritage and culture as distinctive as any in the world. One of these is the Adirondack Mountains, where I live. The rocky land, the freezing winters, and the isolation combined to produce a unique breed of tough, self-reliant settlers and woodsmen in the 1800's.

One of these was the guide and near-hermit Alvah Dunning. Lean, tough, and sometimes downright unsociable, Alvah was legendary for his hunting and tracking skills. He came by these naturally, being the descendant of a famous Revolutionary War scout. In the woods Alvah was always accompanied by at least one of his hounds, rangy nondescript dogs of a kind still popular with old-timers in the Adirondacks.

Alvah, a true man of the woods, never really adjusted to modern life. Though he lived until the turn of the century, he died still firmly convinced that the earth was flat.

To create this carving I worked from old photographs of Alvah, trying to capture not just his physical appearance, but also his fiercely independent personality. I think you'll enjoy the challenge of this carving.

Hole

¼ inch stock

Wire

Grain

Leather Tail

FULL-SIZE PATTERN

Alvah Dunning & Hound

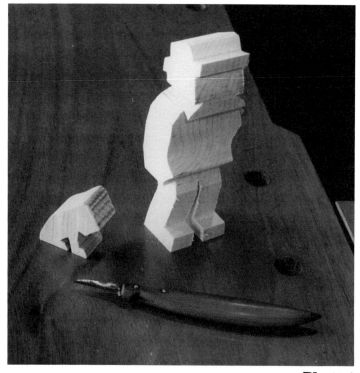

Photo 1

Cut the blank for Alvah Dunning from a piece of air-dried white pine or basswood so that it measures 1¾ in. thick by 2½ in. wide by 6½ in. long. Use a piece 1 in. thick by 2 in. wide by 2 in. long for the hound. Be sure to cut the side profile first on Alvah so the blank will lie flat while you cut the front view. Only cut the side profile on the hound; the rest can be easily whittled out (Photo 1).

Photo 2

Fasten the hound upside down in the vise and use a coping saw to make two cuts about ¼ in. apart to form the front legs. Then whittle out the waste wood between the cuts with a knife (Photo 2). Begin rounding off the back (Photo 3).

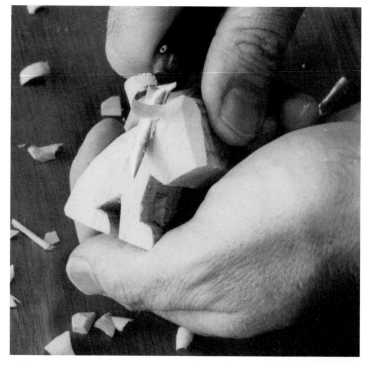

Photo 3

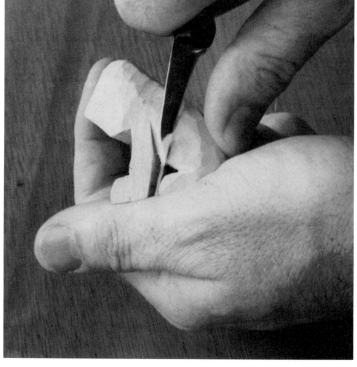

Photo 4

To define the front and back legs, cut a notch by making a shallow vertical cut behind the front leg and then remove the chip by making a paring cut up to it. Do the same thing in front of the rear haunch (Photo 4). Then round off the tummy, legs and haunch.

Alvah Dunning & Hound

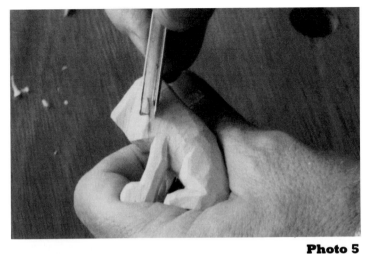

Photo 5

Photo 6

Next, draw on the ears and shape them with the same technique you just used to define the legs. You can also use a V-gouge (Photo 5). Pare away the wood on either side of the V cut to make the ears stand out (Photo 6).

Photo 7

This also shapes the face. Mark the position for the eyes with a pencil, and cut a small notch to form the eye socket (Photo 7). The actual eye will be added later with a drop of paint. Use the V-gouge to incise lines

Photo 8

indicating the nose and mouth (Photo 8). On a dog this small you don't need to carve a lot of detail to capture his personality. In fact, too much detail on a carving of this scale can actually detract from the rustic feeling you're trying to create.

Photo 9

After finishing the face, carve out the space between his hind feet. Then, with the point of your knife "drill" a small hole and glue in a tiny scrap of leather for a tail (Photo 9). I use five-minute epoxy for this job. It forms a strong bond and sets quickly, enabling you to hold the tail in the proper position until the glue hardens. Leather is a better choice than wood for a tail this tiny because it's flexible and won't break off. It also adds a whimsical touch in keeping with this carving's character.

Alvah Dunning & Hound

Photo 10

Now that the hound is finished, you're ready to start on Alvah. The first step is to rough the basic shapes out of the blank. You can do this with a knife, but carving gouges are quicker if you have them.

Fasten Alvah in the vise with the front side up. You will be flattening the stomach, and leaving the right hand slightly raised to hold his rifle. The tool I'm using, called a macaroni gouge, has a square cutting edge, like one-half a small box. The macaroni gouge is somewhat specialized, but you can achieve the same effect by substituting a V-gouge used alternately with a flat gouge. If you have a macaroni gouge though, it removes the wood quickly and easily.

Starting from the left side of the blank, I carve away the ridge by holding the gouge in my left hand and tapping it gently with my right palm (Photo 10). Leave about ½ in. of the ridge to form the right hand.

Photo 11

To shape the arms, pencil in the outline first. Then, using a knife or the macaroni gouge, carefully carve out the inside crook of each arm. Don't try to remove the wood in one big chip; work in from one side and then

the other making a series of V-shaped cuts. Next turn the carving sideways in the vise and rough shape the outside of the arms (Photo 11).

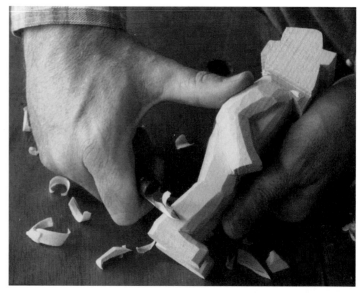

Photo 12

Now you can take Alvah out of the vise. Complete the carving using a knife and small gouges, with Alvah held in your hand.

Start by rounding off all the square corners on the arms and feet (Photo 12). The texture left by the knife cuts suggests Alvah's "rough and ready" clothing. Make sure that all your cuts are with the grain. If the knife starts to dig in, change your grip and remove that chip by carving from the opposite direction.

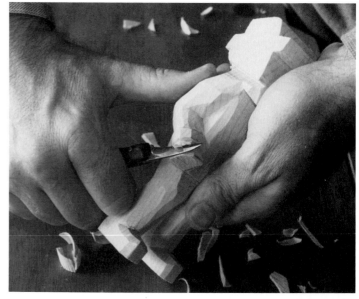

Photo 13

After the arms and legs are rounded, begin the detailing. To make the cuff on the right sleeve, use a V-gouge to make a shallow cut ½ in. from the end of the arm, then make another V cut ¼ in. above that. Pare away the wood above and below the cuff, leaving it raised (Photo 13).

Alvah Dunning & Hound

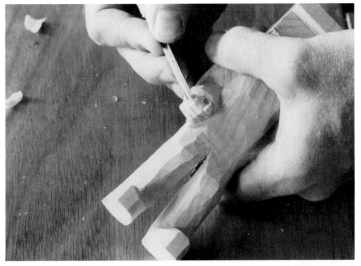

Photo 14

Next, begin working on the face and head. Start by rounding the whole head area above the shoulders into a cylinder. Do this by just rounding off the corners. Do not round the top of the head into a ball shape; leave it flat for now. Draw a line to establish the bottom of the hat brim (Photo 15).

Before shaping the right hand, carefully drill a $\frac{3}{16}$ in. hole through it so Alvah can hold his rifle. Be very careful not to put too much pressure on the hand while you are drilling because the wood can easily split. Let the drill do the work; don't force the bit through the wood. Drill the hole before shaping the hand, because it is less likely to split before the excess is carved away.

After the hole is drilled, shape the major surfaces of the hand. Basically, the fist is box-shaped with the corners rounded off. Look at your own fist to get the general shape, but remember, don't get hung up on the details. Alvah's left hand is conveniently tucked in his pocket, so you only have to carve one.

After the hand is roughed in, carve the thumb by making a line across the top of the fist with the V-gouge, and paring away the wood to leave a raised thumb. To separate the fingers, cut three lines around the fist with the V-gouge (Photo 14).

Make the cuffs around the trousers the same way you did the cuffs on the sleeve. To form the shoes, just round off the corners of the wood on the feet. If you like, you can put a sole on the shoe by incising a very shallow line around the bottom edge of it. This is the same technique used to form the sole of Saint Nicklaus's boots.

Photo 16

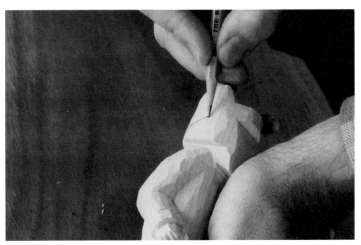

Photo 15

Photo 17

Now start carving the crown of the hat. Make a series of cuts around the top of the hat brim, about $\frac{1}{8}$ in. above the line you just drew (Photo 16). Then cut down from the top to remove the chips and leave the crown standing raised above the brim. Then round the top of the crown (Photo 17). Don't worry about making the hat look smooth; Alvah's hats were always rather battered.

Alvah Dunning & Hound

Photo 18

Next, cut around the lower hat brim with a coping saw, making the cut ¼ in. deep (Photo 18). It's important to shape the hat before making this cut because the hat brim is quite fragile, and might split if the supporting wood below the hat brim were removed first. I use a coping saw instead of a knife for this cut because it puts less pressure on the hat brim than the knife would.

Photo 19

After finishing the saw cut, carve away the excess wood below the hat brim with a knife (Photo 19). Carve toward the saw cut removing small chips and being careful not to put too much pressure on the hat brim. The head should be about 1 in. wide from side to side.

You're now ready to start carving the face. Alvah's face is similar to Saint Nicklaus's, the only real difference is the shape of the beard.

Photo 20

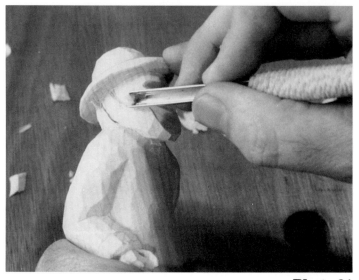

Photo 21

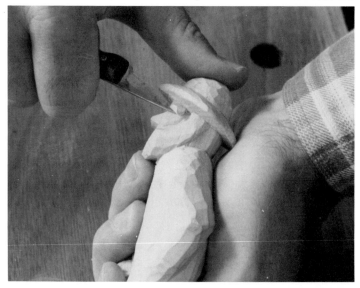

Photo 22

Begin by cutting two notches establishing the eyebrow and nose. The eyebrow notch is ¼ in. below the hat brim, and the second notch, for the nose, is ¼ in. below that (Photo 20). Then draw in two lines on each side of the face for the beard, and incise a shallow cut along them with a V-gouge (Photo 21). Thin down the sides of the face above the beard and shape around the back of the head (Photo 22).

Alvah Dunning & Hound

Photo 23

Detail the nose and eyes using exactly the same techniques as for Saint Nicklaus. With a little practice and experimentation you'll be amazed at the range of expressions and personalities you can create using these basic techniques.

Next, texture Alvah's hair and beard with shallow V cuts. Alvah's mustache is less full and flowing than that of Saint Nicklaus, and I carve it as part of the beard. To finish the face, suggest the mouth with a small V cut (Photo 23).

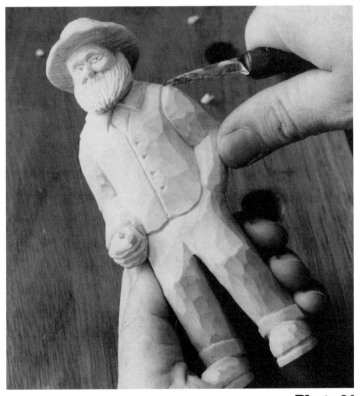

Photo 24

For the finishing details, draw in Alvah's shirt collar, his suede vest, and the edge of the left hand pocket with a pencil. Then go over these lines with a V-gouge, making very shallow cuts. Next pare away the excess wood so that the various items of clothing appear to overlap (Photo 24).

Photo 25

Alvah's rifle is simply whittled from a small scrap of wood ¼ in. thick. Whittle the barrel round and then sand smooth with some 220-grit sandpaper so that it slips easily into the hole in Alvah's hand. If you try to make it fit too tightly you run the risk of splitting the hand. I never glue the rifle in. It usually fits well enough without glue. If the rifle should ever break, it's much easier to replace if it is not glued in.

To add a little more detail to your rifle, you can use two tiny pieces of 18-gauge copper wire for the trigger and trigger guard. Just bend the wires into shape and press them into the soft wood of the rifle with a pair of needle-nosed pliers (Photo 25). You don't need any glue.

Alvah and his hound are painted with the same thinned oil paints as Saint Nicklaus. The hound is painted white with a burnt umber spot. Use a tiny dot of black for each eye. Alvah's hat and vest are painted light tan, a thin mixture of burnt umber and yellow ocher. His shirt is Prussian blue, while his pants are raw umber. The boots are burnt umber. The barrel of the rifle is black, and the stock is burnt umber. Remember to test your paint mixture first on a piece of scrap wood to make sure your colors are the shade you want. Try to keep your color tones soft and muted to avoid a garish look. This method of painting woodcarvings is an excellent way of bringing out the "rough hewn" personality of these characters.

I really enjoy carving these local folk legends. Regional American history is rich with similar individuals: mountain men, prospectors, fishermen, and pioneers to name a few. Give Alvah Dunning a try, and then consider carving some of the colorful characters from your own area. ∎

Full Color Section

Swedish Folk-Art
Doll Horse (page 12)

*Russian Dancing
Bears (page 18)*

St. Nicklaus (page 24)

*Alvah Dunning
& Hound (page 32)*

Salt Box (page 52)

Quilt Rack (page 60)

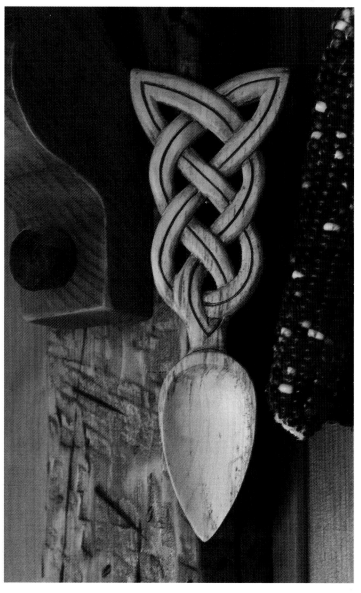

Love Spoon (page 68)

Cardinal (page 74)

Merganser Decoy (page 82)

Lynx (page 88)

Pineapple (page 98)

Thoroughbred Horse (page 104)

Driftwood Troll (page 110)

*Tobacconist's
Indian (page 116)*

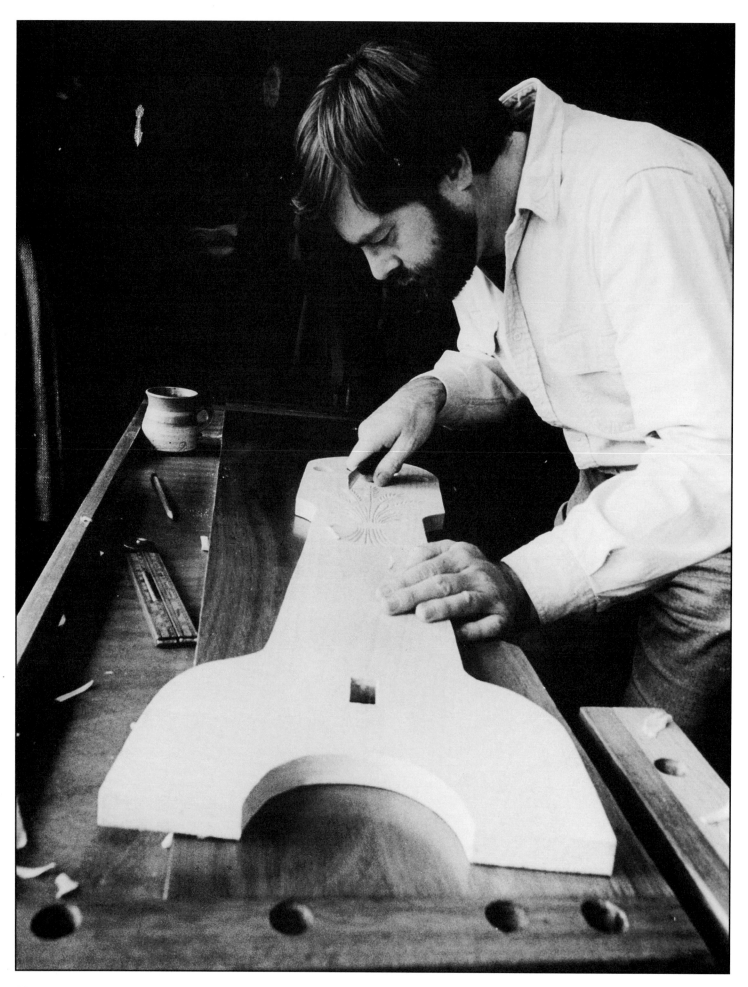

Chapter 3

Chip Carving

Incised carving, where a design is cut down into the surface of a flat board, is common throughout the world. But, in Germany, Switzerland and other Northern European countries, the type of incised carving called chip carving or "kerbschnitzen," has been refined to an art form.

As practiced in these countries, chip carving is extremely versatile. The designs can be simple or astonishingly complex. But, simple or complicated, geometric or free flowing, the carvings are created with the simplest of tools. A knife or two is all the craftsman needs to make hundreds of different designs.

Chip carving is used almost exclusively as a decorative accent on woodworking projects. Cutting boards, jewelry boxes, kitchen utensils and countless other household objects can be enhanced and personalized with the addition of a little chip carving.

So, try some chip carving on your next project. You will discover what folk carvers in the high Alpine valleys have known for generations: that chip carving imparts a warmth and charm to even the simplest household item. The carving goes quickly, and there's a great deal of satisfaction in creating your own chip carved designs. ∎

Salt Box

Color Photo Page 43

Salt Box

oday, salt is cheap and plentiful, so it's easy to forget how precious it was to our ancestors. A salt box like this Early American one would occupy a place of honor in the home, usually near the hearth where heat would protect the salt from moisture.

Like all spices, salt was highly prized as a seasoning. But, salt did more than just enhance the flavor of bland food. Salt also acts as a preservative. Vegetables, fish and meat were either pickled in brine or packed in salt to prevent spoiling.

The chip carving design I chose for this salt box is similar to one a pioneer farmer with only a few tools might have made. The salt box itself is easy to build, and will be a delightful addition to your home.

When I make a project that combines woodworking and carving, I like to do the carving first. That way, a mistake won't spoil the finished piece. Basswood is best for chip carving because of its fine, even grain. Air-dried white pine also works if the design is not too complicated.

Begin by getting out stock for all parts. The Bill of Materials on page 54 provides the finished dimensions of the various parts. Note that the chip carved rosette on the back (B) and front (D) are identical in design, but slightly different in size. The following step-by-step photos show how to lay out and cut the rosette that's on the front of the salt box. While we show the compass being used to lay out the rosette, you could simply use the full-size patterns provided, if you prefer. The compass technique is handy because you can use it to create your own designs.

Photo 2

Photo 3

Photo 1

Because this chip carving design is fairly simple you can lay it out directly on the wood. First, find the center of the board by drawing two diagonal lines from corner to corner (Photo 1). Where the lines intersect is the center of the piece.

Now, using a compass set for a 1½ in. radius, scribe the 3 in. diameter of the rosette. Without changing the setting on the compass, place the point on the bottom edge of the circle, and draw an arc through the circle (Photo 2). At each point where the arc intersects the edge of the circle, draw another arc (Photo 3). Repeating this process will form a six petaled flower design.

Salt Box

Photo 4

Next, set the compass to a 1 in. radius and place the compass point in the center of the larger circle, as shown. Make small arcs halfway between each of the petals (Photo 4). These arcs serve to locate the small

Bill of Materials
(all dimensions actual)

Part	Description	Size	No. Req'd.
A	Bottom	$\frac{1}{2} \times 4\frac{3}{4} \times 7\frac{1}{2}$	1
B	Back	$\frac{1}{2} \times 7 \times 12$	1
C	Side	$\frac{1}{2} \times 3\frac{1}{2} \times 6\frac{3}{4}$	2
D	Front	$\frac{1}{2} \times 4\frac{7}{8} \times 7$	1
E	Lid	$\frac{1}{2} \times 4\frac{1}{4} \times 7\frac{1}{2}$	1

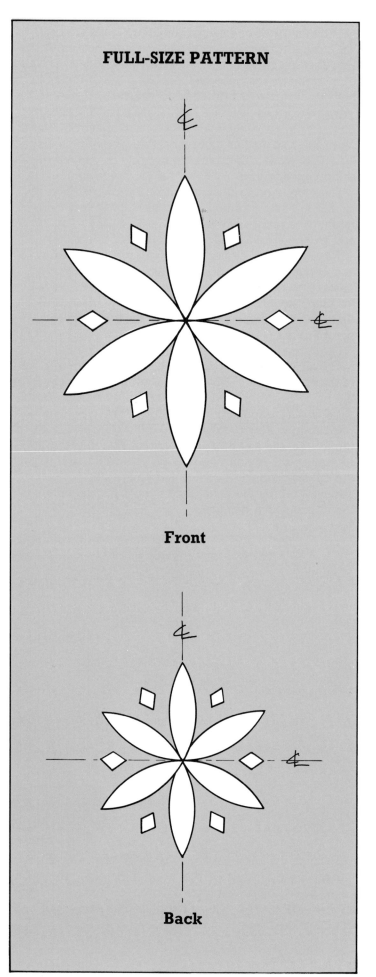

FULL-SIZE PATTERN

Front

Back

Salt Box

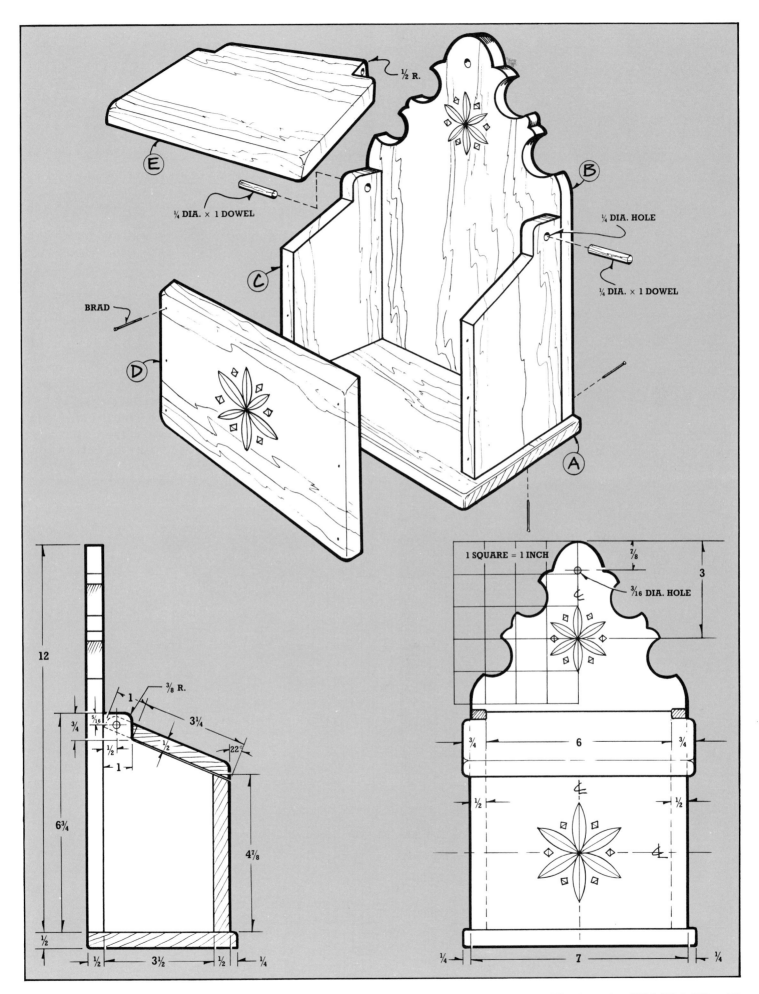

½ R.

E

¼ DIA. × 1 DOWEL

BRAD

D

C

B

¼ DIA. HOLE

¼ DIA. × 1 DOWEL

A

1 SQUARE = 1 INCH

⅞

3

³⁄₁₆ DIA. HOLE

12

³⁄₈ R.

1

1

⁵⁄₁₆

¾

3¼

½

22°

½

1

6¾

4⅞

½

½

3½

½

¼

¾

6

¾

½

½

¼

7

¼

Photo 5

"diamonds" that are part of the design. Using the arcs as a guide, sketch the diamonds freehand (Photo 5).

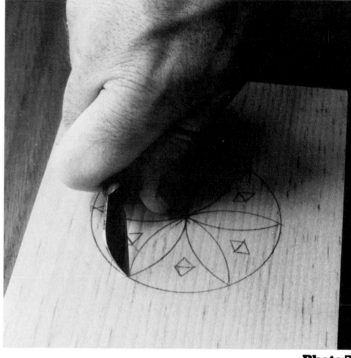

Photo 7

To begin carving, hold the knife with the blade at about a 45-degree angle to the wood, with the knuckles of your hand resting on the wood for support. Then draw the knife through the wood. Make the cut shallow as you begin, gradually deepen it to about $\frac{1}{8}$ in. at the widest point of the petal, and shallow once again at the end (Photo 7).

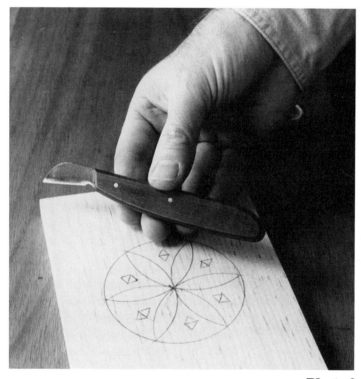

Photo 6

This style of chip carving requires a specialized knife (Photo 6). It has a very thin, sharp blade set into the handle at an angle. The handle is more nearly square than round. The corners serve as a guide for the placement of your fingers. This makes it easier to keep the blade at a consistent angle when you are carving.

Photo 8

After you've made the first cut, rotate the wood 180 degrees and repeat the same type of cut on the other side of the petal (Photo 8). This should remove a nice clean chip. You may want to practice this cut on a piece of scrap wood until you can do it smoothly.

Salt Box

Photo 9

Photo 11

Photo 10

Photo 12

To form the diamonds you use a type of cut called a dreischnitt, which simply means "three cuts" in German. The dreischnitt removes a tiny triangular chip of wood. The diamonds are made up of two dreischnitts back-to-back.

To make the dreischnitt, hold the knife so the blade is perpendicular to the wood. Place the point of the knife at the apex of the triangle and press down making a vertical cut (Photo 9). Repeat this for the other side of the triangle. Then carefully slice out the wood between the two cuts (Photo 10). The dreischnitt should be only about $\frac{1}{16}$ in. deep at its deepest point.

After the front is carved, make the back piece of the salt box. To enlarge the curved back profile, draw a grid of 1 in. squares on a 10 in. by 14 in. sheet of paper. Then transfer the back profile onto this grid pattern (Photo 11). Cut out the design with scissors and trace it onto the back (Photo 12). Then use a coping saw to cut

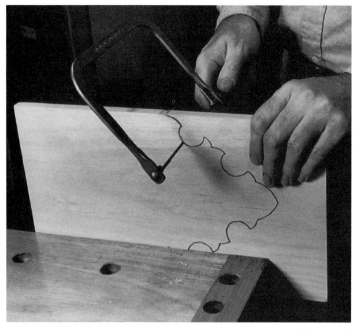

Photo 13

Photo 15

out the design (Photo 13). Use 150-grit sandpaper to smooth the edges and remove any marks from the saw.

If you like, you can also carve a design on the back piece. I used a smaller version of the same chip carving done on the front. Locate the center of the rosette 3 in. down from the top, and draw the outer circle with a 1 in. radius. To mark the position of the diamonds use a ¾ in. radius setting on your compass. The carving steps are exactly the same as for the first rosette.

Assemble the salt box with ⅞ in. wire brads and wood glue (Photo 15). Don't wipe off any glue that squeezes out as you nail the parts together. This would smear it into the pores of the wood, and keep the stain from going on evenly. Wait until the glue dries and remove the excess with sandpaper or a sharp knife.

Photo 14

Photo 16

Next, cut out the remaining parts of the box. Use a coping saw to notch the sides and lid. Drill a ¼ in. diameter hole in each side piece to form the hinge for the lid. Photo 14 shows the parts carved, cut out, and ready for assembly.

Hand plane the top edge of the front to match the slope of the sides (Photo 16). While you have the plane out, round the top rear edge of the lid. That way the corner won't bind when the lid is open.

Salt Box

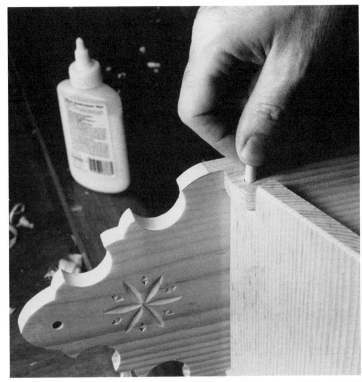

Photo 17

Photo 18

To make the hinge, first place the lid in position on the salt box. Then, using the holes in the sides as a guide, drill a ¼ in. diameter hole ½ in. deep into each side of the lid. Now cut two 1 in. long pieces from ¼ in. diameter dowel rod. Put the lid in position and test fit the dowels in the holes. You may have to sand the dowels down a little bit so they fit smoothly. If the fit is too tight you won't be able to open the lid.

Use a toothpick to place a drop of wood glue at the bottom of the dowel holes in the lid. Locate the lid and slide the dowels into position (Photo 17). If any excess dowel sticks out beyond the side of the salt box, whittle it off with a knife and sand it smooth.

For the finishing touches, bevel the front edge of the lid slightly with the hand plane. Then check the whole salt box, and smooth off any sharp edges and corners with 150-grit sandpaper. Sand very gently over the carvings with a 220-grit sandpaper wrapped around a flat sanding block to remove any pencil marks. The sanding block will help prevent rounding the edges of the carving and blurring the design.

The salt box looks more antique if you stain it to darken the wood. I used Wood Finish by Minwax in Special Walnut. Apply the stain with a 1 in. paintbrush and wipe it off promptly (Photo 18). A little of the stain will remain in the carvings and make the design stand out.

You may not need a place to store salt in your home, but I'm sure you'll find this little box handy for dozens of household odds and ends. ■

Quilt Rack

Color Photo Page 44

Quilt Rack

A handmade quilt has always been a work of special beauty, and deserves a place of honor in the home. This quilt rack provides the perfect way to display and protect your heirloom quilts when they are not in use.

I really like this particular design because of its simple, clean lines. It is not difficult to make, even with traditional hand tools, and would be an enjoyable project by itself. But a little decorative carving really completes the project and gives it a finished look.

I've chosen the classic sheaf of wheat design to decorate this quilt rack. Wheat is a symbol of fruitfulness and abundance, and it adds a warm country accent. The wheat pattern is chip carved using techniques similar to those we used on the Salt Box.

If you like, you may substitute other chip carving designs that appeal to you. The large flat surfaces of the quilt rack are perfect for a variety of chip carved patterns. And, on page 67 I've included a traditional Alpine flower pattern that you might like to try. The carving techniques are the same as those described for the sheaf of wheat.

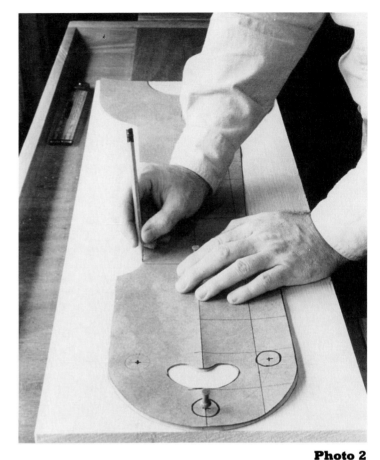

Photo 2

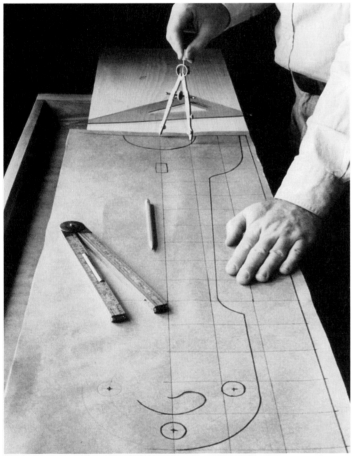

Photo 1

Enlarge the quilt rack pattern to full size using the grid as a guide. Draw one half of the pattern on a large sheet of paper, then fold the paper in half and cut out the pattern (Photo 1). This will give you a template for the ends (A).

Photo 3

Trace the pattern onto a piece of pine that measures ¾ in. thick by 11¼ in. wide by 32 in. long (Photo 2). Cut it out with a band saw; then use a spokeshave to smooth the edges (Photo 3). Use a rasp and sandpaper to smooth the curved sections.

Quilt Rack

Quilt Rack

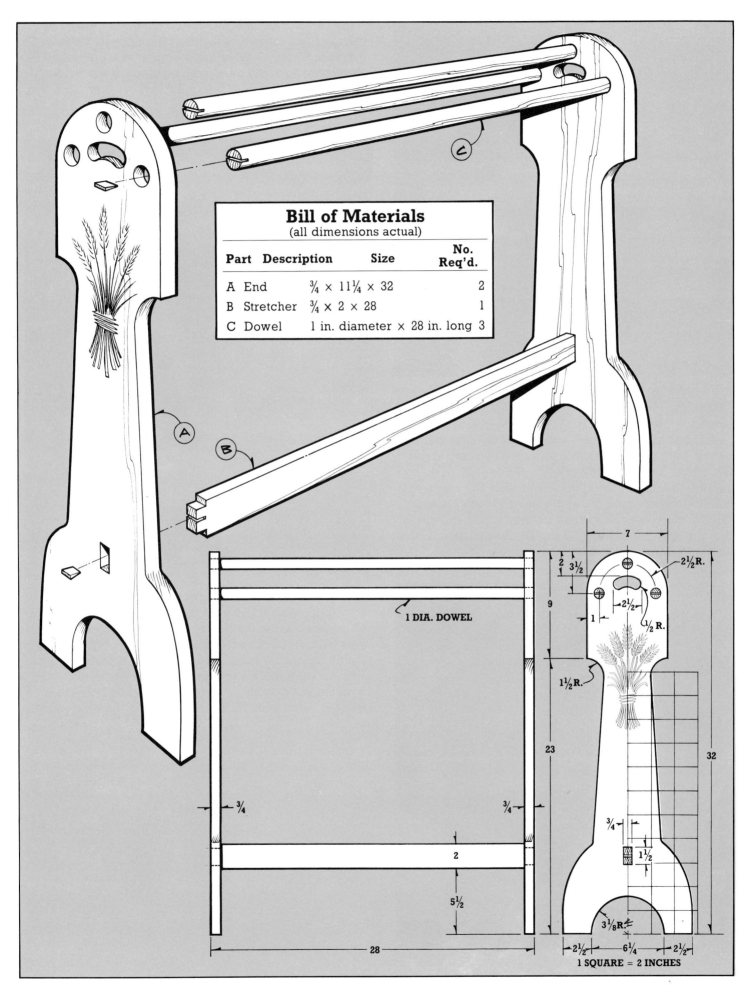

Bill of Materials
(all dimensions actual)

Part	Description	Size	No. Req'd.
A	End	¾ × 11¼ × 32	2
B	Stretcher	¾ × 2 × 28	1
C	Dowel	1 in. diameter × 28 in. long	3

1 DIA. DOWEL

1 SQUARE = 2 INCHES

Quilt Rack

Drill a 1 in. diameter hole for each end of the hand grip and in each location where the dowels will be inserted (Photo 4). Then use a coping saw to remove the excess wood in the hand grip between the two holes you drilled (Photo 5). Smooth the inside of the hand grip with a rasp and sandpaper.

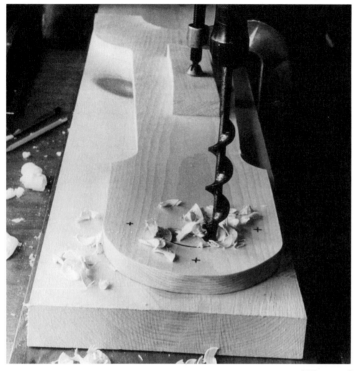

Photo 4

Next, mark the position of the hand grip and the centers of the dowel holes. Put a piece of scrap wood underneath the end piece, before you fasten it to the bench, to protect your work surface. The scrap wood also helps prevent splinters when the drill bit goes through the other side of the board. Use a C clamp to hold the wood down. It's also a good idea to place a small cushion block between the end piece and the C clamp when you fasten it down. This keeps the clamp from making indentations in the soft pine.

Photo 6

To make the mortise, or rectangular hole, for the stretcher (B), drill two ¾ in. holes through the wood. Then take out the excess wood with a flat carpenter's chisel (Photo 6). This tool has a bevel on only one side, which leaves the other side of the blade perfectly flat. This makes a more accurate vertical cut than a woodcarver's chisel, which is beveled on both sides. Use the same techniques to make the other end piece.

Photo 5

Quilt Rack

Photo 9

Photo 7

Photo 8

Photo 10

Next, make the stretcher. The stretcher fits between the bottom of the end pieces and gives the quilt rack strength and stability. Cut the narrow section (called a tenon), at each end of the stretcher to fit into the mortise holes made earlier. Use a thin-bladed saw like a dovetail saw or a Japanese crosscut saw. Make the vertical cut first (Photo 7). Then make a horizontal cut to remove the chip (Photo 8). While the stretcher is in the vise, make a saw cut down the center of the tenon for the wedge (Photo 9).

After completing the stretcher, cut the dowels (C) to the correct length and slot their ends for the wedges. Make sure the slots are running in the same direction on both ends of each dowel. Dry fit the entire quilt rack together to make sure all the pieces fit properly before you begin carving.

Use carbon paper to transfer the wheat pattern to the ends, then start carving the individual grains of wheat. Use the angled Swiss chip carving knife to incise the wheat grains the same way the "petals" were carved on the Salt Box. That is, make a cut along one side of the wheat grain angled inward at 45 degrees. Then make a second cut along the opposite side, also angled inward at 45 degrees, to meet the first (Photo 10). This removes a neat seed-shaped chip.

Quilt Rack

Photo 11

Next, carve the band that binds the sheaf of wheat together, using the same type of cut. Remember to keep your knuckles braced on the wood for support. This helps you keep the blade at a consistent angle.

Again, use the same cut to form the wheat stalks. Try to cut the entire length of the stalk in one smooth cut for a flowing line. Then, make a similar cut on the other side of the stalk to remove the chip (Photo 11). This can be a tricky cut to master. But go slowly, and once you get the feel of it, you'll find that it gives a clean, crisp look to your carvings.

Photo 12

Carve the lower end of the wheat stalks the same way, with one exception. Before you make the long sweeping cuts along the sides, make a short vertical stop cut at the bottom of the stalk (Photo 12). This will make the stalks end sharply, as though they had been cut with a scythe.

Photo 13

After you have finished carving both ends of the quilt rack, remove any marks left by the carbon paper using a soft cloth moistened with lacquer thinner. If any marks still remain, sand them off gently with 220-grit paper. Be sure to use a sanding block to avoid blurring your design.

Before assembling the quilt rack, make the eight wedges needed to lock the stretcher and dowels. The wedges are thin, tapered pieces cut from a scrap of hardwood. I used beech wedges made from a piece of firewood for this quilt rack. You'll need six wedges that are 1 in. wide for the dowels and two wedges ¾ in. wide for the stretcher. Make them about 2 in. long, and tapered from 3/16 in. at the thick end down to a pointed edge. It's a good idea to test fit the wedges in the holes in the end pieces to make sure they go through easily. If they bind in the holes they may exert too much sideways pressure and split the wood.

The slots in the dowels and the stretcher should be arranged so that the wedges go in horizontally, that is, perpendicular to the vertical wood grain. If they were aligned vertically, that is parallel to the wood grain, they could split the wood when pressure is applied.

Quilt Rack

Now you are ready to assemble the quilt rack. Spread a thin coat of wood glue on the ends of the dowels and tenons. Wipe a little glue around the inside surfaces of the holes too. Then fit the pieces together.

To insert the wedges, first place the quilt rack on its side. Put a thin layer of wood glue on the wedges and tap them in snugly with a mallet (Photo 13). When all the wedges are inserted, use a fine-bladed saw to cut off each one just above the surface (Photo 14). If you cut too close to the surface, you may accidentally mar the wood. Use a no. 3 gouge to pare the protruding end until it is flush. Let the glue dry overnight for maximum strength.

You can finish the quilt rack with any stain or varnish that will match the rest of your furniture. I used Minwax Puritan Pine Wood Finish on mine, and then polished it with their paste finishing wax. This buffed to a warm, mellow sheen that blends well with the wood in my log cabin.

This quilt rack is a project any quilter will be proud to display their work on. It's a great looking addition to your home, and useful, too. ■

Photo 14

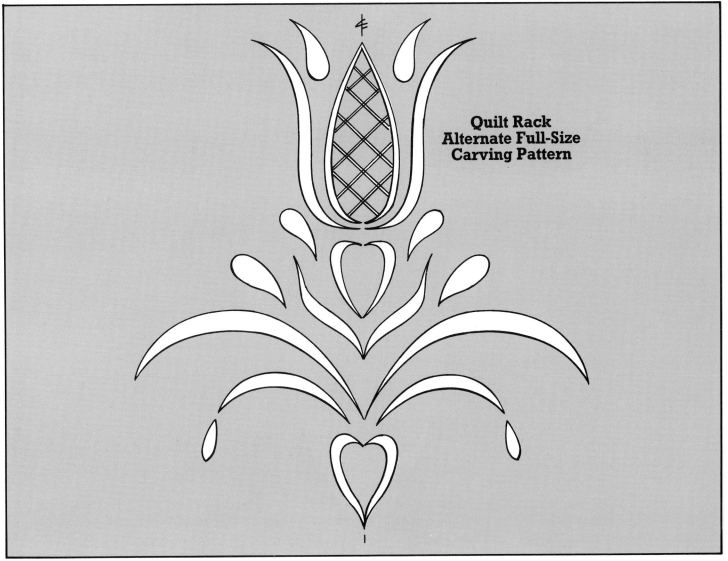

**Quilt Rack
Alternate Full-Size
Carving Pattern**

Love Spoon

Color Photo Page 44

Love Spoon

Spoons are considered symbols of affection in many cultures. In Wales for example, in times past, a young man would present a decorative hand carved spoon to the girl he wished to marry. The fine finish and intricate design of the carving reflected his affection for her. If she accepted his gift, they were considered betrothed.

While the love spoon tradition dates back at least 300 years, the handle design on this particular spoon is far more ancient. It is an example of Celtic knotwork. These interwoven designs, thousands of years old, are etched into stone artifacts and appear throughout Ireland and parts of Britain. The pattern on this spoon forms one continuous loop symbolizing the togetherness and loyalty of the couple.

Photo 1

To begin, trace the full-size pattern on a basswood blank measuring ⅜ in. thick by 3¼ in. wide by 9 in. long (Photo 1). It will be helpful to draw the design on the back as well as the front. Remove the pattern, and carefully sketch the lines indicating how the bands intertwine. Then cut the outline of the love spoon with a band saw or coping saw.

Photo 2

The next step is to drill holes through the handle for the pierced design. Fasten the spoon blank to the bench with a large C-clamp. Put a piece of scrap wood between the blank and the bench top to protect the bench from the drill. The scrap wood will also keep the holes from splintering on the back. Use a ¼ in. drill bit to establish these holes (Photo 2).

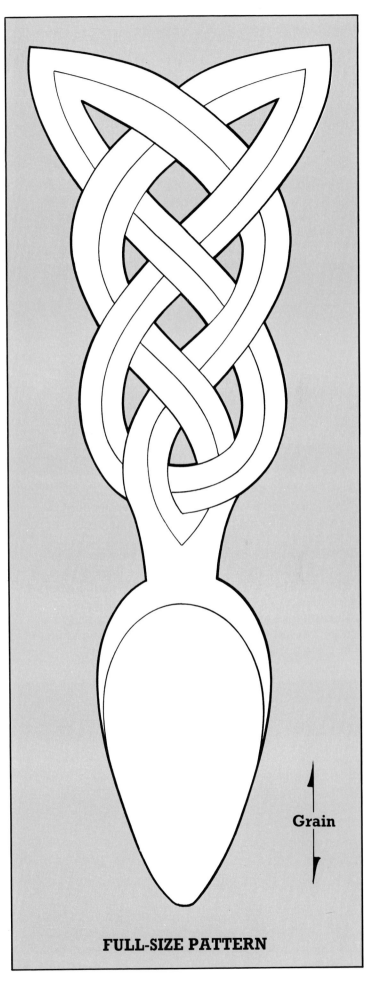

Grain

FULL-SIZE PATTERN

Love Spoon

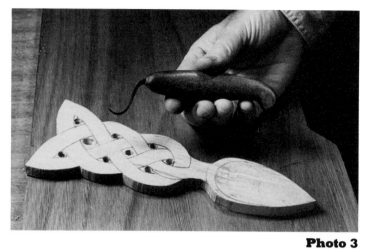

Photo 3

Photo 4

Use the straight-bladed knife to round the back of the bowl (Photo 5). Be careful not to take off too much wood and accidentally put a hole through the spoon. One way to check your progress is to hold the spoon up to a strong light. If you can see light through the bowl of the spoon, you don't need to remove any more wood.

When you have shaped the bowl of the spoon, sand it smooth with 150-grit sandpaper. Finish sand with 220-grit paper.

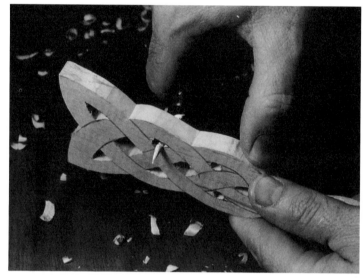

Photo 6

To hollow out the bowl of the spoon, you could use gouges, but the more traditional tool is a curved Welsh knife called a "twca cam." The curved knife that I sometimes use for carving wildlife is very similar to it (Photo 3). While twca cam knives were usually custom made, and are no longer available, a 1⅛ in. diameter Swedish carver's hook also works well for this hollowing operation. Use the same kind of paring cut that you would with a straight-bladed whittling knife to scoop out the excess wood (Photo 4).

Next, shape the holes in the handle. Insert a thin-bladed knife into the drill holes and carefully cut out the excess wood (Photo 6). Make the corners of the holes nice and crisp. A small triangular file is handy for cleaning out any rough spots.

Photo 5

Photo 7

To create the illusion that the intertwining bands of the handle actually overlap, cut notches to suggest that one band goes over the other. Chip carving techniques can be used to make these notches. Holding the chip carving knife vertically, cut down about ¹⁄₁₆ in. along the edge of the raised band (Photo 7). Don't go any deeper, or the handle may become too fragile. Next, use the paring cut to remove the chip (Photo 8).

Love Spoon

Photo 8

Once you have finished the front of the spoon, you can turn it over and carve the intertwining bands on the back. Before you start, carefully check your design to make sure the bands are overlapping the right way. For example, a band that is on the top in front, should appear to be underneath the band it crosses from the back. Getting this detail right really enhances the illusion that the bands cross each other.

Photo 9

After you have finished the overlapping bands, bevel the edges with a knife to round them slightly (Photo 9). Then sand the handle smooth with 220-grit sandpaper. I prefer garnet paper because the garnet crystals fracture as you sand, continually exposing a fresh cutting surface. Garnet is a natural semi-precious gemstone mined in the Adirondacks. It was first used for sandpaper in the 1700's.

Be careful when you sand not to round the notches you cut earlier. These cuts need to remain well-defined to maintain the illusion that the bands actually interweave.

To further enhance the design, you can incise a groove down the center of each band. Use the chip carving knife to make two cuts at a 45-degree angle to the wood (Photo 10).

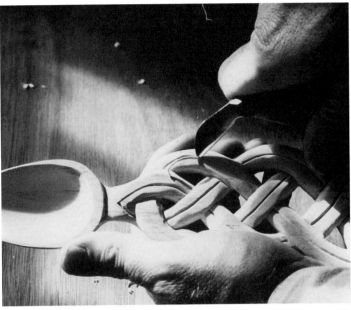

Photo 10

Ordinarily, you shouldn't sand a piece before carving it because particles of abrasive embedded in the wood will dull your tools. However, in this case the surface of the wood needs to be smooth so you can make a clean cut. The uneven surface left by the tool marks would make the groove appear ragged.

Photo 11

In Wales, a spoon made for everyday use would be boiled in water after it was carved, to remove the sap. Then it would be rubbed with salt to whiten and harden it. Love spoons, being purely decorative, were seldom treated this way. Since this spoon won't be used for food, I recommend a clear finish like linseed oil or Wood Finish by Minwax in Natural (Photo 11). After the finish has dried, add a light coat of paste wax. This adds a touch of shine to accent the shapes.

Today a love spoon makes a charming gift for any occasion. It will look terrific hanging on the kitchen wall or next to a fireplace. ■

Chapter 4

Wildlife Carving

Wildlife carving challenges your carving skills in new ways. But wildlife carving is more than an exercise in technical expertise. It is also a way to gain a greater appreciation of the natural world and the creatures we share it with.

To capture the spirit of an animal in wood, you need to understand the animal first. Careful observation of the creature in the wild will give you a feeling for its personality and its way of moving. All this will be reflected in the lifelike quality of your carvings.

Learning more about wildlife will also enhance your enjoyment of the outdoors. You will find, as I did, that when you look at a bird or animal with the thought of carving it someday, you will notice so much more. You will see subtle colors, the shape of a wing against the sky, the shine of soft fur in the sun — details a casual glance might miss entirely.

The carvings you make from your observations can be any style you choose. They can be sleekly stylized or meticulously realistic. As long as the basic shapes and characteristic poses are right, the carving will radiate life and personality. These three projects are an opportunity for you to give wildlife carving a try. A project such as the Merganser illustrates that you need not include a great deal of detail to capture a creature's character. After familiarizing yourself with wildlife carving techniques you can carve some of the creatures you observe first hand, such as the birds that visit your feeder on cold winter mornings. Your carving skills will increase along with your appreciation of the natural world. ■

Cardinal

Cardinal

The cardinal is one of the best loved American song-birds. Its brilliant red plumage has made it the state bird of seven different states.

Once primarily a southern bird, cardinals have moved steadily northward. This is a result of more people setting up winter bird feeders, enabling the cardinal to survive in colder latitudes.

Having grown up in the Midwest, I enjoy a special love for cardinals. As a boy I raised an orphan nestling until he was old enough to survive on his own. This experience gave me a special appreciation for the cardinal's cheerful song and unique personality. I remember many summer mornings brightened by their clear call of "cheer-cheer-cheer" echoing from the hedges and distant fence posts surrounding the lush green cornfields. So, whenever I hear their song today, I am reminded of those times and the pleasant memories.

This cardinal is a straightforward carving project. It requires few tools, and you'll find it a good introduction to the joys of wildlife carving.

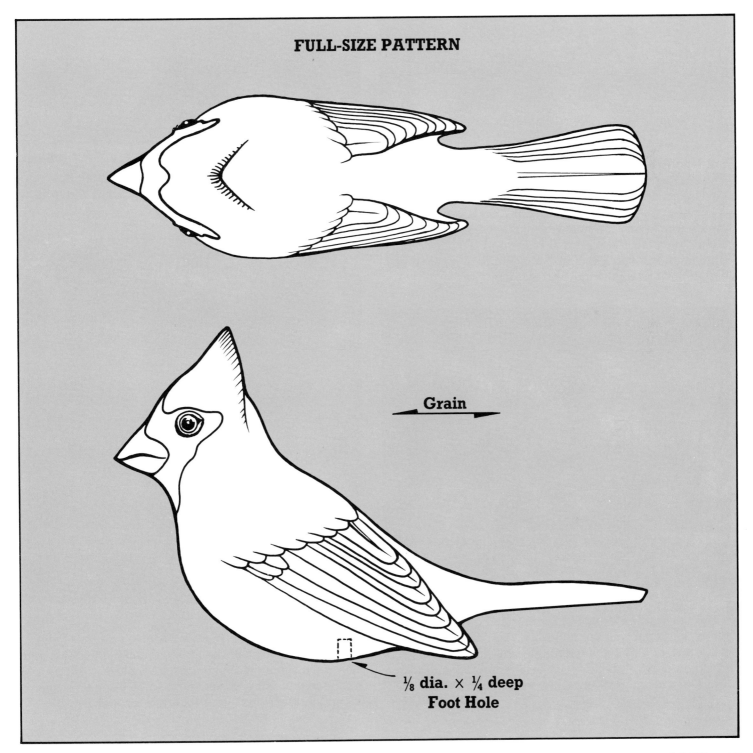

FULL-SIZE PATTERN

Grain

⅛ dia. × ¼ deep
Foot Hole

Cardinal

Photo 1

The tools I use on a project like this are my carving knife, a 6 mm V-gouge, and a 7 mm no. 5 gouge with a curved shaft. The curved shaft of the no. 5 gouge makes it easier to get into tight spots. A tiny no. 8 gouge is handy for carving the holes to set the eyes (Photo 1). Either air-dried white pine or basswood is a good choice for this carving. You'll need a piece measuring 1¾ in. thick by 4 in. wide by 6 in. long.

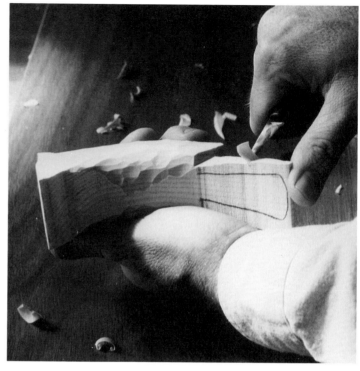

Photo 3

Thin the tail, and remember to leave the wing tips broader than the tail. Don't remove much wood from them at this point (Photo 3).

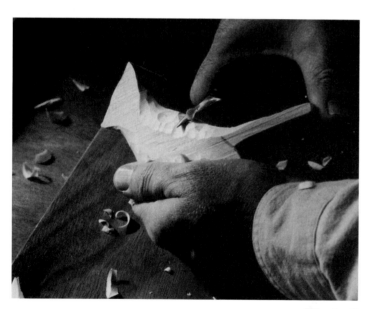

Photo 2

Lay out the side profile of the cardinal on the carving blank, cut it out with the bandsaw, and then pencil in the top view. Begin the carving by rounding off the sharp corners. Birds are very sleek, rounded animals, and you want to avoid a blocky look (Photo 2).

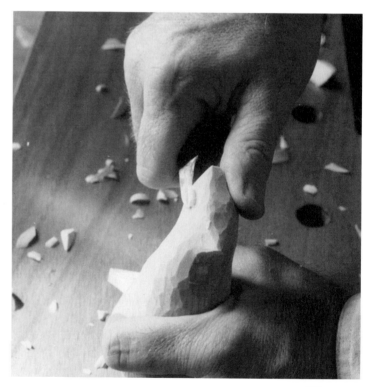

Photo 4

Next, thin the head (Photo 4). A bird's head is quite narrow. The cardinal's head is pointed at the beak, and also at the tip of the crest in back. The crest will be fragile because it is cross-grain, so be gentle carving around it. Make sure your tools are razor sharp.

Cardinal

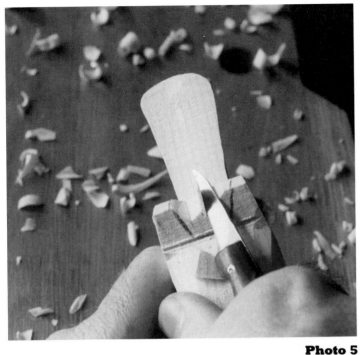

Photo 5

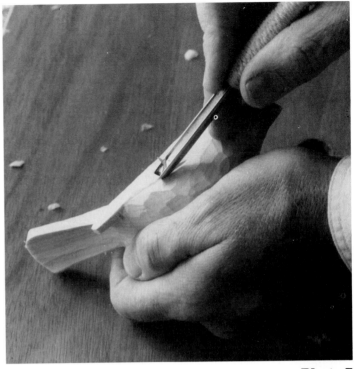

Photo 7

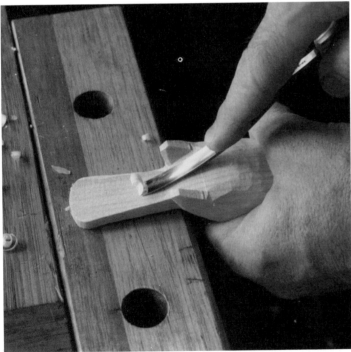

Photo 6

Photo 8

After removing most of the excess wood from the blank, you're ready to start carving some of the details. First, mark out the wing tips on the underside of the bird. Use your knife to remove the excess wood between the wings (Photo 5). The wing tips are fragile, so take out the waste wood in several stages rather than all at once. Use the no. 5 gouge to smooth the area between the rump and the tail, and make the underside of the tail slightly concave (Photo 6). Brace the carving on the bench for greater control.

Pencil a line for the lower edge of the wing, and incise a cut along it with the V-gouge (Photo 7). Then pare away the wood below the V-cut to round the tummy. Incise another line with the V-gouge to outline the top edge of the wing where it lies along the back. The dropped wing pose is very characteristic of the male cardinal. Now pare away the wood between the wings with the knife (Photo 8).

Cardinal

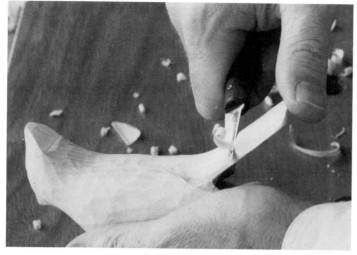

Photo 11

Using the no. 5 bent gouge and the knife, undercut the back of the crest slightly and shape the back of the head (Photo 11). This will help give the crest a light, feathery appearance. Remember, the crest is fragile so take off small chips and don't put too much pressure on the wood. In fact, before you start carving these details, it would be a good idea to make sure your tools are extra sharp. A sharp tool will leave nice, clean cuts and make shaping the face much easier.

You can now begin putting in the feather texture. On a small carving like this, I indicate most of the feather texture with the paintbrush. However, for the coarse feathers of the crest and the larger feathers of the wings and tail, some detailing adds to the realism. While this can be done using a small V-gouge and a knife, a woodburning pen is quicker and more efficient.

Photo 9

Thin the upper side of the tail with the knife (Photo 9). Watch the direction of the grain carefully while you are carving. Because of the shape of the tail, it's easy to find yourself going against the grain. If the wood starts splintering, approach the cut from the opposite direction. This will prevent accidentally splitting off the tip of the tail.

After establishing the basic shapes of the wing tips and tail, go ahead and remove the excess wood. The secret of making the feathers look delicate, while still being strong, is to make the edges thin but leave the center portion thicker.

Now begin detailing the head. First thin the shape of the head a little more. Then draw the line that separates the beak from the face. On a cardinal, the transition between the feathers on the face and the beak is very smooth. This line is just to guide you in shaping the beak. Also draw a line separating the upper and lower mandible (the top and bottom halves of the beak).

Don't make the beak too thin. A cardinal's beak is large and powerful for cracking seeds. Some reference photos, if you have them, will help to detail the beak. Better yet, if cardinals live in your area, observe them at your bird feeder.

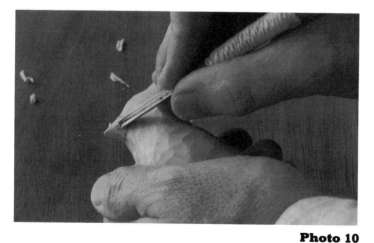

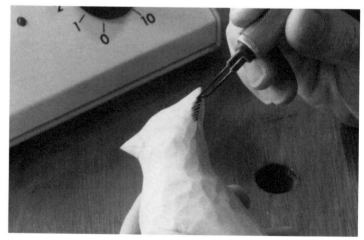

Photo 12

The woodburning pen I use is called a Detail Master II. It has interchangeable tips in a variety of shapes and sizes, and a regulator dial to control the temperature.

To detail the crest feathers, use a narrow skew shaped tip. With the heat setting on medium, scorch in a series of fine lines to simulate the ends of the crest feathers (Photo 12). It's helpful to first test the temperature of your tip on a scrap of the same wood the cardinal is carved from. Different woods, and even the same type of wood from two different trees, can require varying amounts of heat to achieve the same effect.

Photo 10

Make a very shallow cut with the V-gouge along the line you have drawn between the upper and lower halves of the beak (Photo 10).

Cardinal

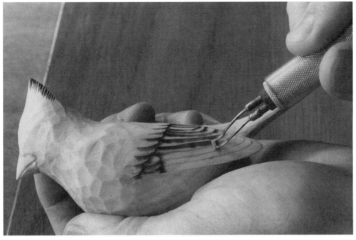

Photo 13

Before you burn in the flight and tail feathers, use a piece of fine 220-grit sandpaper to lightly sand your bird. Use a very light touch. You don't want to remove the tool marks, since they add to the soft feathery look of the completed bird. Just soften their edges slightly. The wings and tail should be sanded smoother than the rest of the body, to facilitate burning in the details. Lightly pencil in the outlines of the wing and tail feathers. Don't worry about counting the number of feathers. Normally songbirds have up to 20 flight feathers, but when the wings are folded — as in this pose — many of them are hidden by overlapping.

Use a straight tip in the woodburning pen to establish the wing and tail feathers. Hold the tip almost flat against the wood, tilting it down slightly toward the outer edges, and carefully outline the feathers (Photo 13). The heat causes the wood to shrink, leaving the feather edge slightly raised. Don't forget, the feathers on the top of the back lie over the lower ones like the shingles on a roof.

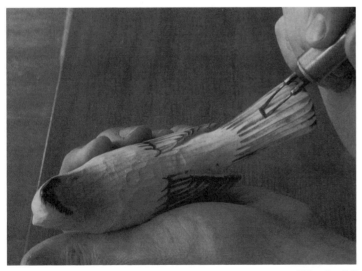

Photo 14

Burn in the tail feathers using the same technique. Start with the middle tail feather on the upper side of the tail, and then do the feathers on either side. For added detail you can use the same technique to burn in a central shaft on the middle feather (Photo 14). Next

burn in the feathers on the underside of the tail (Photo 15). Remember, they overlap in the opposite direction, so the middle feather will be almost hidden by the others. Burning-in is a useful technique for adding detail to your carvings. It just takes a little practice with the woodburning tool to learn how to control the depth and evenness of your lines.

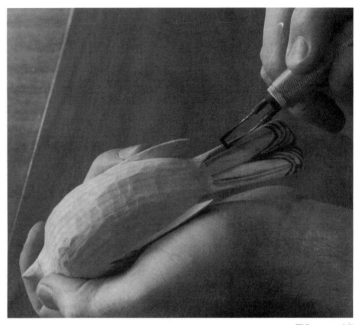

Photo 15

After detailing the crest and feathers, brush or spray a thin coat of lacquer on your carving. This seals the wood for added protection against moisture. The lacquer also provides a smoother painting surface. I use Deft Clear Wood Finish spray lacquer in an aerosol can.

When the lacquer is dry, add the eyes. The eyes I use are clear glass with a black pupil (see Sources of Supply index). They come in a large variety of sizes. Use a 6 mm eye on the cardinal. The backs of the glass eyes are painted to match the eye color of the bird species you are carving. Cardinal's eyes are dark brown, and burnt umber works fine for this color. Use acrylic paint because it dries quickly and adheres well to the glass.

First, carefully draw the eyes on the carving. Be sure they are in the same position on both sides of the head. Nothing will spoil the look of your finished cardinal more quickly than having one eye higher or lower than the other. Also make sure they are set back the same distance from the beak. Reference photos will help you determine the correct position.

I find that drill bits, even ones designed to cut smoothly, always tear the wood on the face a little, so I recommend using a small gouge to make the eye hole. With a gouge you can control the size, depth and position of the hole more accurately. The tool I use to set in the eyes of small songbirds like the cardinal is a 3 mm no. 8 woodcarving gouge.

Cardinal

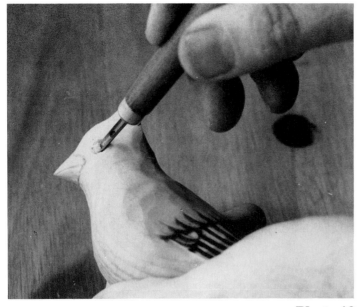

Photo 16

Use the gouge to carefully scoop out the wood inside the circles you have drawn for the eyes (Photo 16). Occasionally test fit the eye to make sure the hole is large and deep enough. The eye should set well down in the socket to avoid a "bug-eyed" look on your finished carving.

Photo 17

Epoxy putty works best to glue the eyes in. It has a thick clay-like consistency that hardens to form a socket. It can also be used to form a realistic eyelid around the eye. The epoxy comes in two parts that react chemically and harden when they are mixed together. To set the cardinal's eyes you only need a tiny amount. Take a piece the size of a pea of each component and mix them thoroughly. The putty will not harden unless it is mixed completely.

Place a small ball of putty in the eye socket and gently press the eye into it. Some putty will ooze out around

the eye as you press it in. This putty is used to form the eyelid.

To shape the eyelid, first remove any extra putty, leaving just a small ring of it around the eye. Then shape the putty to form the eyelid. A small flat toothpick is ideal for working the putty (Photo 17).

It takes the putty an hour or two to harden. When it has cured, paint a base coat of white gesso on the entire carving, except the beak and eyes. Gesso is used by artists to prime their canvases. It creates a good surface to paint on, and the white base coat allows the feather colors to show up clear and true.

The one problem in painting a carving like this is holding it while it is wet. I make a holding stick by taking a piece of wood 1 in. square and 7 in. long. Drill a hole in one end and glue the head of a no. 6 wood screw about 1½ in. long into it with epoxy putty. Secure the point of the screw into the underside of the bird, preferably at the location where one of the holes will later be drilled for the leg. This holding stick makes a perfect handle.

Photo 18

The paints I have found to work best for wildlife carvings are Griffin alkyd colors (see Sources of Supply index). Alkyd paints are very similar to oil paints but dry in only a few hours.

The cardinal's color scheme is wonderfully simple. The basic color is cadmium red medium. The mask around the eyes and beak is ivory black. Before you start painting, outline the black areas with a pencil.

Use a no. 6 flat synthetic sable brush to paint on the red. When you apply the paint, try to make your brush strokes follow in the direction the feathers grow. That is, from the head toward the tail. This textures the paint and, when dry, helps create the illusion of actual feathers (Photo 18).

Cardinal

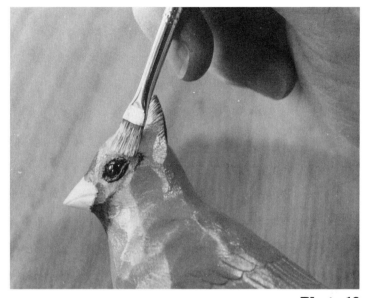

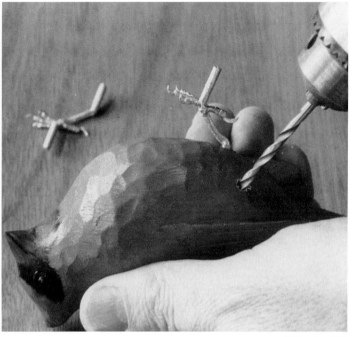

Photo 19

Paint the black mask with a smaller no. 4 pointed brush. To make the cardinal look feathery use a Grumbacher no. 2 flat bristle brush to lightly blend the black paint over the red (Photo 19). Use a very light touch and wipe the brush clean after each stroke. You want tiny lines of black brushed over the red to suggest overlapping feathers. This is a wet-on-wet technique, but you don't want the black and red paints to mix. This would create an unpleasant "muddy" look.

Paint the beak with a mixture of cadmium red and a tiny bit of burnt umber. Use a no. 4 pointed brush and paint on a very thin layer — just enough paint to color the wood.

When the paint is dry you're ready to mount the bird. The base I chose for this carving is the top of an old fence post. Cardinals are often seen perching on fence posts along the edges of pastures and meadows. You could also use a piece of driftwood or a small section of stump.

The first step in mounting a bird is to insert the legs. You can make legs and feet out of wire, or you can buy cast feet from a woodcarving supply company (see Sources of Supply index). These are made of a flexible mixture of lead and pewter, so you can mount your cardinal in a realistic pose.

Lightly mark the position of the legs on the underside of the cardinal with a pencil. Drill two small holes ¼ in. deep to accept the legs (Photo 20). For this set of legs I used a ⅛ in. diameter drill bit.

Don't glue the legs in yet. I have found it's best to first fit the legs into their holes without gluing them. Then hold the cardinal in position on the base and mark where to drill the holes for the central peg on each foot. Then drill the peg holes, and fit the whole carving together before gluing anything. This insures that your carving will sit perfectly on its base.

When you're happy with the way the pieces fit together, glue the legs in place with five-minute epoxy. Then paint them brown with burnt umber acrylic paint. It may take two coats for complete coverage.

Photo 20

Photo 21

Now glue the cardinal to the base with five-minute epoxy. Hold the bird in place until the glue dries (Photo 21). After the glue has dried you'll want to do some final detailing. Use red paint to touch up any spots around the holes drilled for the legs, where the paint may have chipped off. Bend the feet so that the claws appear to be gripping the base, and touch up any places where metal shows through the paint.

Don't hurry through the mounting of your carving. A little extra time spent on this step will make a difference in how well the finished piece looks.

I have always found songbird carving to be one of my favorite styles of woodcarving. It's very enjoyable and satisfying, and the work goes along quickly. Try the cardinal or choose your own favorite backyard songbird for your model. I think you'll have a lot of fun! ■

Merganser Decoy

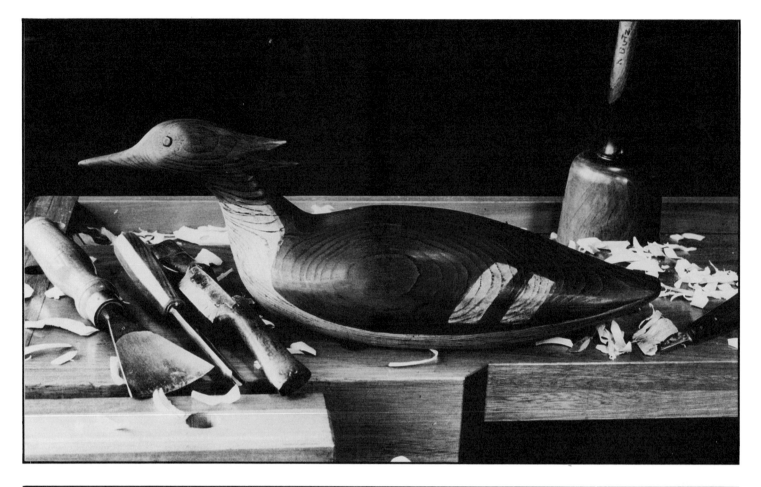

Color Photo Page 45

Merganser

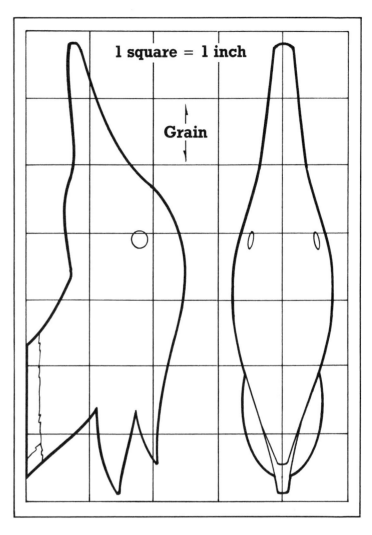

1 square = 1 inch

Grain

This project is a different kind of wildlife carving. It is a reproduction of the type of handmade solid-body decoy first created around the time of the Civil War. They were popular until the turn of the century when factories began mass producing commercial decoys.

The beauty of these early carvings is the simplicity of the design. Each one expresses the individual artistic vision of its creator. Once merely a hunting accessory, today these decoys are prized by collectors and recognized as an important folk art.

This particular decoy is my own design — based on a style popular in the 1880's, and on my own observations of mergansers. It captures the feeling of the female common merganser in her energetic pursuit of fish.

Perhaps the real pleasure of making a woodcarving like this is the absence of realistic detail. It's an opportunity to just go with your feelings as you shape the wood.

White pine was the traditional wood used for this type of decoy. It worked easily, floated well, and the resin in the wood made it somewhat water resistant. You could use a solid block for the body, but I prefer to laminate it from two pieces of wood. A laminated block is less likely to split from internal stresses in the wood. Also, the thinner wood is easier to find today, and less expensive.

Photo 1

Cut the two pieces for the top and bottom of the body so that each piece is about 1⅝ in. thick by 6½ in. wide by 13½ in. long. Make sure the grain runs lengthwise in both pieces. Cut the head from a piece 1⅝ in. thick by 3 in. wide by 7½ in. long. The grain should run the length of the head for maximum strength in the beak and crest (Photo 1).

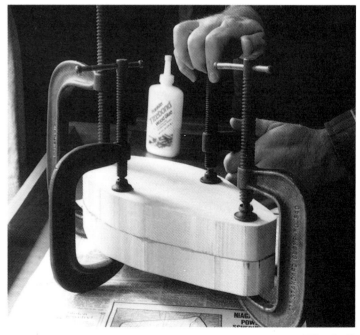

Photo 2

Glue the top and bottom sections of the body together with wood glue. Clamp the pieces together until the glue dries (Photo 2). Put a piece of newspaper on your bench to protect the surface from the excess glue that will squeeze out as you tighten the clamps.

Merganser

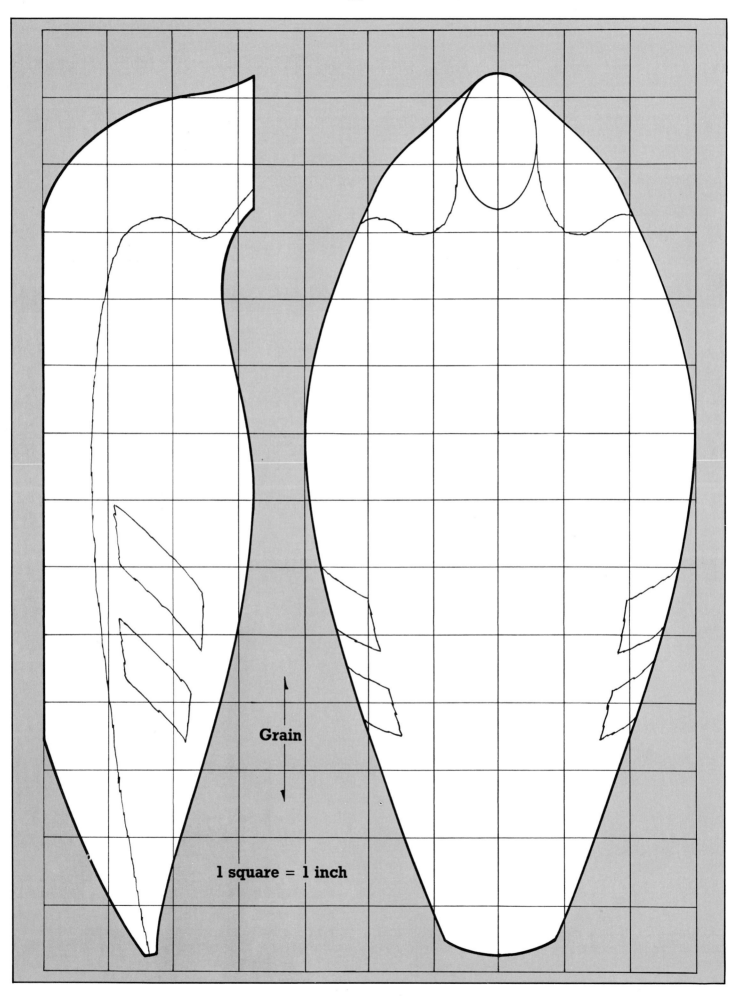

Grain

1 square = 1 inch

Merganser

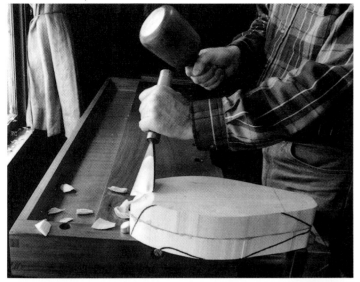

Photo 3

Photo 5

Photo 4

Photo 6

Use the same large gouge that you used on the bottom to shape down the tail section. Then use a 15 mm no. 9 gouge and carve out the hollow behind the neck (Photo 6). Use the 30 mm. no. 2 gouge to smooth the back where it slopes down to the neck.

When the glue dries, remove the clamps and sketch the side view of the merganser. The first step in carving is to remove the waste wood. Fasten the block upside-down to the bench, and draw a center line along the bottom to serve as a guide in getting both sides even. Select the largest gouge you have. In this case I'm using a 60 mm no. 6 fishtail to remove the wood quickly (Photo 3). Don't worry about following the lines of the pattern exactly. Most of the old decoy makers didn't use patterns; they just shaped it by eye. While the block is fastened to the bench, go ahead and round off the sharp angles of the bottom. A 30 mm no. 2 gouge works well for this step (Photo 4). Leave a flat spot on the bottom so the decoy will sit on your fireplace mantle without tipping over.

Now you're ready to turn the body over and start shaping the top. The rounded base can make the body difficult to hold in the vise, so I use a hardwood holding block. This one is made from a piece of oak, 2½ in. thick by 3 in. square. Drill two holes in it so a pair of 3 in. long wood screws can fit through easily. Screw the block to the base of your carving (Photo 5). The block is then clamped in the bench vise. This system holds your carving very efficiently.

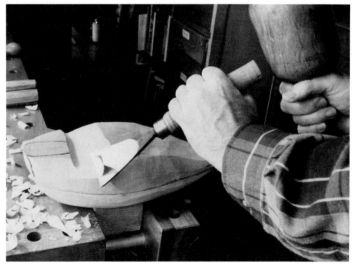

Photo 7

Next, draw a center line down the back and mark where the head will meet the neck section. Then use the large gouge to round the back (Photo 7). Be sure to leave a flat area where the head will be glued on.

Merganser

Photo 8

For the final smoothing you can use a spokeshave — just as the original decoy makers did (Photo 8). If you don't have a spokeshave you can use a flat gouge like a no. 2 to smooth the body.

Photo 9

The head is a straightforward whittling project. Just remember, the cross section of a merganser's bill is rounded, rather than flat like other ducks. Use your carving knife to shape the head. Begin by rounding the square angles of the block. Then narrow the crest and bill (Photo 9). Don't worry about too many details, just make the shape smooth and streamlined. After all, the old decoy makers didn't put in any more detail than was necessary to fool a duck.

Next, glue the head on, making sure the gluing surfaces are flat and smooth. I used five-minute epoxy for this because you can hold the head in position while the glue sets. Although the epoxy hardens in under 10 minutes, you should allow a couple of hours for it to cure and reach maximum strength before continuing work on the decoy.

Once the glue cures, take a knife and shape the area where the neck joins the body (Photo 10). You can touch up any rough spots that remain with a piece of 180-grit sandpaper.

Photo 10

Photo 11

Now, you could paint your decoy at this stage. But I prefer to first add the appearance of several decades of weathering. The quickest way I have found to do this is to scorch the wood with a propane torch (Photo 11). Be sure to work outdoors. Light the torch tip and, holding it 3 to 6 in. away, slowly and evenly move the flame along the wood. Don't let the wood actually burn. Just try to create an overall dark brown color.

Photo 12

Then take a stiff wire brush and clean off the charred wood (Photo 12). The heat from the flame will lightly char the softer wood between the annual growth rings. When brushed away, it accentuates the grain pattern, simulating years of hard use.

When scorching the merganser, the heat may cause the glue joint to loosen slightly. If you encounter this problem, just work a little more glue into the joint and let it dry. Don't worry if the seam shows a little. It will only make your decoy look more antique.

Use acrylic paint to color the merganser. For the chest and underparts, mix a little burnt umber with white to make a light gray. Apply the paint with a large flat bristle brush like a no. 8. The paint darkens when applied to the bird because the scorched wood shows through. This adds to the antique look.

Merganser

Photo 13

While you've got the white paint out, add the diagonal stripes on the wings. Use a smaller brush like a no. 4 for this step. Then paint the wings a medium brown. For this color, mix burnt umber and white with a little ultramarine blue. Next paint the head a rusty red. The color I used is red oxide (Photo 13).

The painting on the merganser is very stylized. It only shows the broad areas of color that you would see if you were viewing the bird from a considerable distance. The old decoy makers didn't worry about too much detail, and the ducks didn't seem to notice the difference.

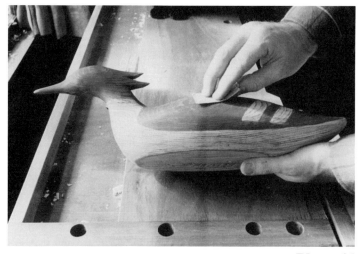

Photo 14

To give the paint a weathered look, take a piece of 220-grit sandpaper and lightly sand the painted carving. This removes some of the paint from the ridges left by the wire brush. Go slowly with this step and sand very lightly. You don't want to take off much of the paint, just enough to give the carving a weather-beaten look (Photo 14).

After sanding, attach the eyes. You could use glass eyes like we did with the cardinal, but for an old style decoy like this, black upholstery tacks are more authentic (Photo 15). Support the head from the back with your hand so that it doesn't break off when you tack in the eyes.

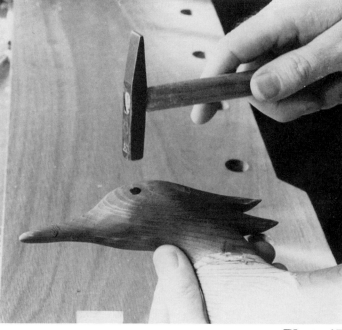

Photo 15

Photo 16

For the final touch, brush a light coat of brown stain on the merganser, and wipe it off immediately (Photo 16). The stain darkens the exposed wood and mutes the paint colors slightly. It also brings out the grain of the wood. Special Walnut Wood Finish by Minwax works well for this. I use paper towels for wiping and dispose of them in a metal container as soon as I'm finished with them. This avoids the fire hazard of having oily rags lying around. I think you'll be surprised at the nicely weathered feeling this technique creates — and so will your friends.

I really enjoyed making this carving. Its antique appearance combined with the modern streamlined shape makes a dramatic sculptural form.

But please don't use this decoy for hunting mergansers. I happen to enjoy their silly antics — and besides, they taste terrible. ∎

Lynx

Color Photo Page 46

Lynx

The lynx is not a creature you are ever likely to find in your backyard. In the few areas lynx still inhabit, they are shy and elusive, seldom seen by even the most patient observer.

This year, I was fortunate enough to have a unique opportunity to study lynx. And, I couldn't pass up the chance of carving one.

The lynx is a medium-sized wildcat, similar in appearance to its cousin the bobcat. Lynx prefer a more northern climate than bobcats and so are found mainly in Canada and the high mountain regions in the United States. In these areas the lynx's long legs and enormous furry feet give it a distinct advantage in hunting its favorite prey, the snowshoe hare, through deep snow.

Never common, lynx have become a symbol of the untamed northern wilderness. Only the most remote areas, virtually untouched by the hand of man, can support a healthy lynx population. The presence of lynx in its traditional habitat is a sign that the country's essential wild character has been preserved.

The lynx is a challenging wildlife carving project, requiring patience and close attention to detail. In fact, I wouldn't recommend it until you've had some other wildlife carving experience. When you do try the lynx I believe you'll find the final result well worth the effort.

FULL-SIZE PATTERN

Grain

Photo 1

You'll need a carving blank 3¼ in. thick by 7½ in. wide by 6¼ in. long for the lynx. I used air-dried white pine and achieved the 3¼ in. thickness by laminating two 1⅝ in. thick pieces together. Lay out the side profile on your carving blank, with the grain oriented vertically. Then cut out the side profile either with the band saw or by hand using a coping saw. Now draw in the front, top and bottom profiles. The remaining carving is all done by hand with gouges (Photo 1).

Begin carving by fastening the blank in the vise and using a 35 mm no. 5 gouge to round the back. Thin down the tail area somewhat, but don't take off too much wood at this point. The tail is cross grain and will be fragile. Detailing it will be one of the last steps of the carving process.

Lynx

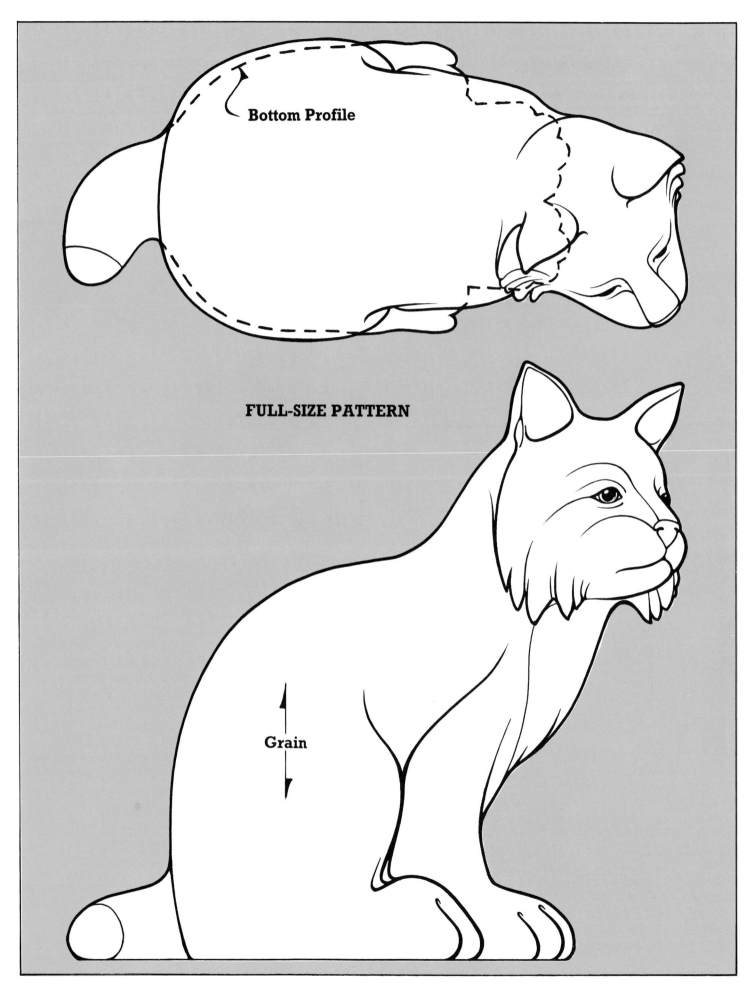

Bottom Profile

FULL-SIZE PATTERN

Grain

Lynx

Photo 2

Photo 3

Use a large V-gouge like a 12 mm no. 14 to outline the haunch and hind foot (Photo 2). Then pare down the wood that forms the front legs (Photo 3).

Next, carve away the excess wood in front of the ears with a 30 mm no. 2 gouge. Remember, at this stage, just rough out the general shapes of the head to help you visualize its position in the wood. Don't take off too much wood; the shapes will be refined later. Also remove some of the excess wood on the face (Photo 4).

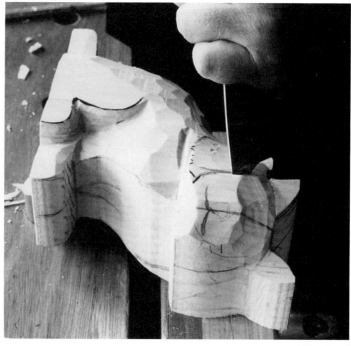

Photo 4

Before you begin shaping the face it would be helpful to refer to some photographs of lynx and other wildcats. If you have a pet cat, study its head carefully. The lynx's head is more massive, but the general shapes are very similar. It is important to take some time and work these shapes out carefully because the position and angle of the head determine the whole pose of the cat.

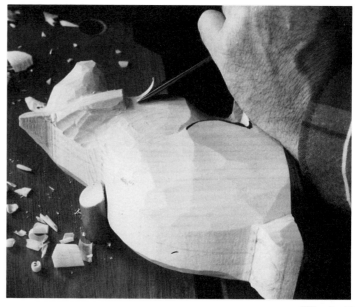

Photo 5

After the head is blocked out, work back from it to shape the shoulders and haunches. Use the 30 mm no. 2 gouge to round the shoulders (Photo 5). You can use the same gouge to shape the haunch. For smoothing over a rounded surface you can reverse the tool so the bottom of the blade is facing up (Photo 6). The curve of the gouge matches the curved shape of the back. This technique works best with a gouge that has a shallow sweep, like a no. 2 or 3.

Lynx

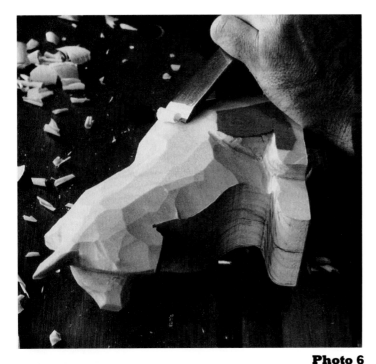

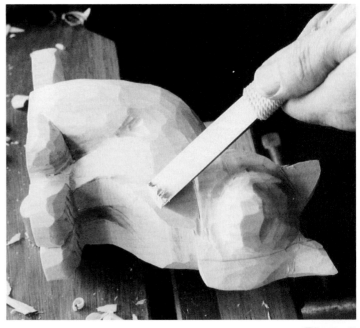

Photo 6

Photo 8

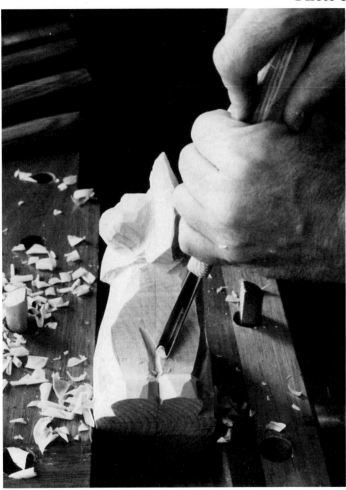

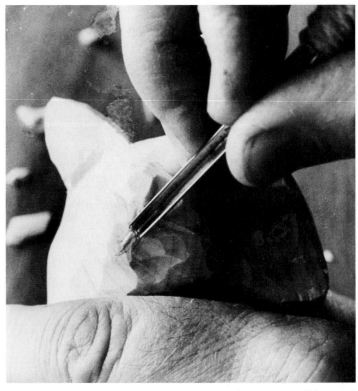

Photo 9

After the body is shaped, it's time to detail the face. Use a sharp knife and carefully whittle out the shapes. Take your time and keep checking to make sure you have the expression you want. Use a small V-gouge like a 3 mm no. 12 to carve the shape of the mouth (Photo 9).

Photo 7

Use a V-gouge to define the shapes of the front legs (Photo 7). Then outline the profile of the front legs with the V-gouge and pare away the excess with a 16 mm no. 2 gouge (Photo 8). Use a knife to round the legs and tail.

Lynx

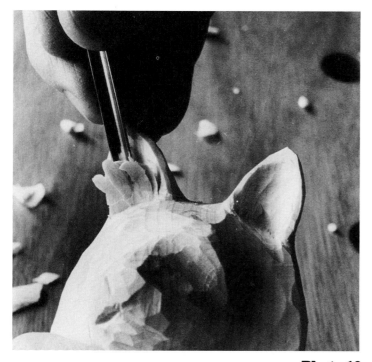

Photo 10

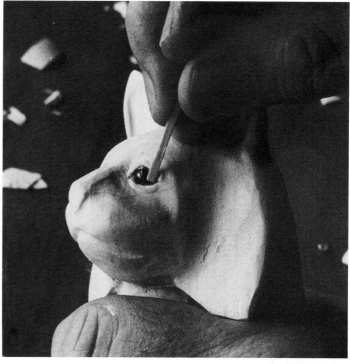

Photo 12

Next, hollow the ears with a 4 mm no. 8 gouge (Photo 10). You don't need to remove a lot of wood, since this will make the ears too fragile. Make the edges thin, but leave the center thicker. The illusion of depth will be enhanced later with paint.

Reference photos are helpful in getting the facial details exactly right. When the face is carved, lightly sand it with 220-grit sandpaper.

Set the eyes in place with epoxy putty using the same technique as on the cardinal. The only major difference is in the shape of the eyelid. A mammal's eye is more almond shaped that a bird's. Use a little extra putty and a toothpick to form this shape (Photo 12).

Photo 11

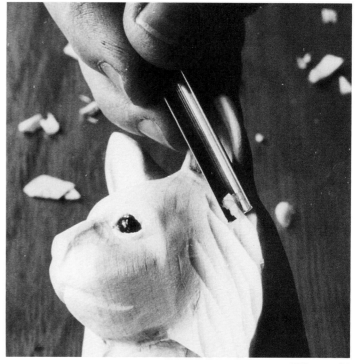

Photo 13

The next step is to set in the eyes. Use a 3 mm no. 8 gouge to carve a small hole to accept the eye (Photo 11). I selected 7 mm glass eyes and painted the back of the eyes light yellow with acrylic paint. Mix yellow ocher light with cadmium yellow deep, and a little titanium white to make the correct shade.

After the eyes are in place, take a 9 mm no. 7 gouge and texture the wood with tool marks that follow the direction of fur growth on a lynx (Photo 13). Later when the hairs are etched in with a woodburning pen the gouge marks will give the feeling of the lynx's thick, shaggy, winter fur.

Lynx

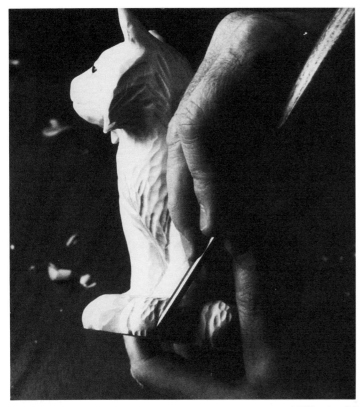

Photo 14

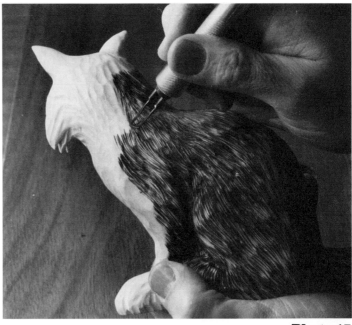

Photo 15

Photo 16

The lynx has feet that are huge in proportion to its body. This, combined with their covering of thick, fluffy fur allows the lynx to run quickly over deep snow without sinking in. Use a 3 mm V-gouge to make three shallow cuts on the front paws to suggest toes (Photo 14). The claws do not show in this carving because they are fully retracted and hidden by thick fur.

Now that the lynx is completely textured, sand lightly with 220-grit paper all over to soften the sharp ridges of the tool marks. Don't over sand and remove too much texture.

To create a realistic coat of fur for the lynx, use a woodburning pen. I use a Detail Master II with a narrow skew-shaped tip. Pencil in some lines indicating the direction of hair growth to guide you in texturing the fur. Set the heat regulator at a medium temperature to begin. Be sure and have a scrap of wood handy to test the temperature before you start. You want to burn in a line that is deep brown in color. If the lines are black, you are charring the wood and your tip is too hot. If the color is very light tan, the tip is too cool.

You may have to adjust the temperature occasionally as you work because the hardness of the wood varies in different areas. For example, end grain requires a higher temperature.

To help suggest the direction of the hair growth, start at the rear and work forward. This creates the impression of hair overlapping from the head to the tail. On the body of the cat the strokes are about ½ in. long. Don't make them all perfectly straight; curve them slightly to follow the contours of the body and the direction of hair growth (Photo 15). On the face, make the strokes shorter to suggest finer hair (Photo 16).

After the lynx is completely burned-in, seal the wood with lacquer. I don't recommend a brushing lacquer for this step. It would go on too heavily and fill the fine lines left by the woodburning tool. Instead, apply a thin coat with an aerosol spray like Deft Clear Wood Finish.

The lacquer will create a good surface for painting. It prevents the water-based acrylic paint used on this carving from soaking into the wood too deeply.

Now apply a base coat of yellow ocher mixed with a little titanium white. Thin the paint with water and apply it in transparent coats with a stiff brush like a no. 3 China bristle. This will allow some of the color of the woodburning to show through the paint and add depth and texture to the lynx's coat. On the chest, lower face, ruffs and inside the ears, apply a thin wash of white instead of the yellow ocher mixture.

Lynx

Photo 17

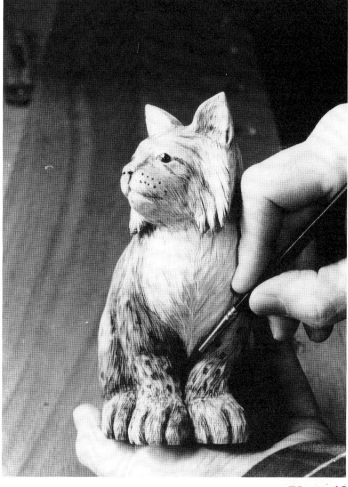

Photo 18

Photo 19

After the base coat has dried, add dark spots with a no. 4 synthetic sable brush (Photo 17). The color I used is ivory black blended with a little burnt umber to warm it. Thin the paint slightly with water and apply it sparingly. A thick coat of paint would fill in the fine lines of the fur texture. Don't make the spots too large or dark. A lynx has more subtle markings than a bobcat. The tip of the tail is also dark.

For an added touch of realism you can shade the recessed areas of the lynx. Use a very thin wash of burnt umber and darken the shadow areas slightly (Photo 18). To make the nose pinkish, add a thin wash of burnt sienna to the very tip.

The final detail on the lynx is the whiskers. Like all members of the cat family they have long sensitive whiskers. These aid the lynx in moving safely through thick, tangled underbrush. To insert the whiskers, first cut several 1½ in. long bristles from a small house painting brush. Next take a needle and poke two holes about $\frac{1}{16}$ in. deep on each side of the muzzle. Mix some five-minute epoxy. Pick up a tiny drop of the glue on the point of the needle and place some into each of the holes. Use tweezers to insert two or three bristles in each hole (Photo 19). Let the glue dry thoroughly.

You can leave your lynx freestanding or mount him on a piece of driftwood with five-minute epoxy. Either way you will have a carving that brings the spirit of the wilderness into your home. ■

Chapter 5

Relief Carving

Relief carving is similar to chip carving in that both methods are used mainly to decorate or embellish flat surfaces. However, instead of the designs being incised down into the wood, relief carving utilizes a technique where the background is cut away, leaving the main elements raised above the surface. Then the raised portions are shaped and detailed. This is all done with a variety of carving gouges. Whether the design is simple or complex, the technique used to create a relief carving is basically the same.

Just about any picture that you can draw, you can carve in relief. However, because you are working essentially in two dimensions, you need to put some extra thought into creating the illusion of depth in your carvings. I'll cover some of the basic methods that are used to create this illusion of depth in the four relief carving projects.

One of the things I enjoy most about relief carving is the chance to use a wide variety of carving gouges. There is a very real satisfaction in using a tool that hasn't changed in centuries. It gives you a feeling of touching the past and continuing a time-honored craft. You'll have a chance to discover this feeling for yourself when you begin working through the projects that follow. ■

Pineapple

Color Photo Page 46

Pineapple

The pineapple is a traditional symbol of hospitality in New England. Odd as this sounds at first, there is a very good reason for it. During the 1800's New England was the hub of a vast seafaring trade network. Sea captains from the area roamed the oceans, sometimes for years at a stretch. When they returned they brought exotic gifts for their friends and family. And, with its freezing winters, what could be rarer in New England than tropical fruit, especially pineapples. Some captains even placed pineapples in front of their homes as a sign that they had returned and visitors were welcome.

Eventually, carved wooden pineapples took the place of the real thing. A carved pineapple on the door is still a sign that a hearty welcome awaits within.

This pineapple is essentially a relief carving with the background completely removed. It's a good project with which to start relief carving because it requires few tools. I used only three different gouges and my whittling knife for the whole carving.

The original hospitality pineapples were carved from pine. Pine was light, easy to work, and best of all, plentiful. New England's thriving ship building trade provided a nearly endless supply of scrap pine for decorative carving. In keeping with tradition I chose pine for this carving.

Photo 2

To hold the pineapple so that you can work on it, first fasten it to a flat piece of wood. I used a piece of ⅜ in. thick plywood cut 14 in. square. Drill two ¼ in. diameter holes through the plywood, and screw the pineapple to it with two 1¼ in. long flathead screws. Plywood is a good choice for this because it doesn't split. Then fasten the plywood to the bench with C-clamps. This is a very efficient arrangement because you can easily turn the carving around to work on it from different directions just by loosening the clamps and repositioning the board.

Photo 1

To begin, trace the profile of the pineapple on a piece of air-dried white pine that is 1⅝ in. thick by 5½ in. wide by 9 in. long (Photo 1). Next, cut this profile out with a bow saw (Photo 2). You could use a band saw, but a bow saw is more traditional. When I make a historic project like this, I really enjoy using the same type of tools that the original makers used. It gives me a feeling of being in touch with the past.

Photo 3

The first step in making the carving is to round over the general shapes. Use a 35 mm no. 5 gouge to rough out the pineapple (Photo 3). Be careful not to put too much pressure on the leaves as you carve. The leaf tips are cross-grain and could break off.

Pineapple

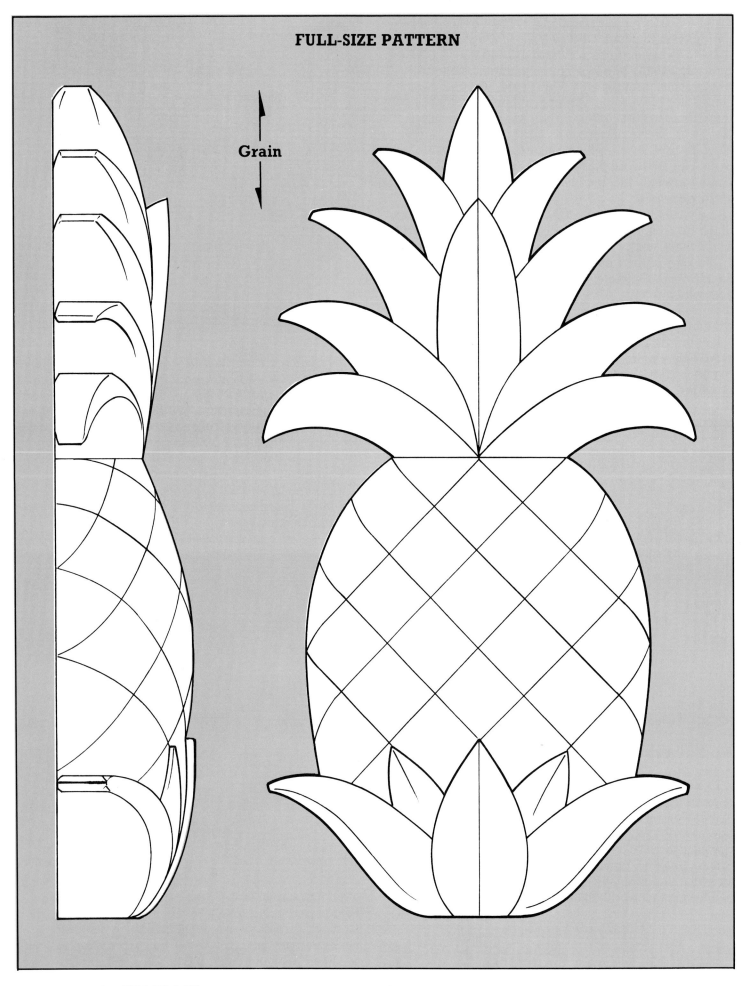

FULL-SIZE PATTERN

Grain

FULL-SIZE PATTERN

Pineapple

Photo 4

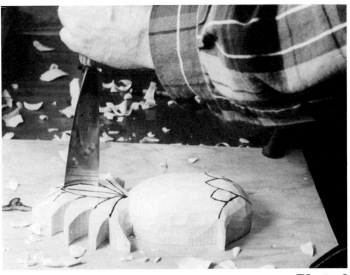

Photo 6

Use the same gouge to cut a large notch between the top of the pineapple and the leaves (Photo 4). Cut first from one side and then the other to remove the excess wood.

Photo 5

Photo 7

After the basic shapes are roughed out, draw the leaves (Photo 5). Don't worry about making them perfectly symmetrical. In fact, your carving will look more authentic if there are some slight irregularities in the design.

Next, make a cut straight down about ⅛ in. deep along the outline of the center leaf with the 35 mm no. 5 gouge (Photo 6). The curve of this particular gouge matches the curve of the leaf. In relief carving, this step is called "setting-in."

Photo 8

Then, use the same tool to bevel down the wood on either side of the center leaf, leaving it raised (Photo 7). Set-in the other leaves the same way. When all the vertical cuts are made, use the 35 mm no. 5 gouge to bevel the bottom edge of each leaf (Photo 8). This will make the leaves appear to overlap.

Pineapple

Photo 11

Photo 9

Use the same techniques to lower the base of the center leaf so that it appears to come out from behind the other leaves. It's best to shape this lower part of the leaf first, because the surrounding leaf edges are delicate and can be accidentally chipped off by too much pressure. Then finish shaping the leaf by beveling down either side of the top section (Photo 9).

There are many different ways to create the texture of the pineapple's skin but the one I like best is a cross-hatched pattern. Its simplicity shows up well from a distance. Begin by sketching in diagonal lines about ¾ in. apart. The lines wrap all the way around the sides of the pineapple. Once again, don't worry about making these perfect. Strict mathematical precision isn't necessary, and might even detract from the overall effect.

Use a 6 mm V-gouge to make cuts along the diagonal lines (Photo 11). Then remove the pineapple from the board.

Photo 12

Photo 10

To shape the bottom leaves, first use the 35 mm no. 5 gouge to set-in the center leaf and the two large side leaves, just as you did with the top leaves. Then set-in the two smaller leaves with a 20 mm no. 5 fishtail gouge. When all the bottom leaves are set-in, use the 20 mm no. 5 fishtail gouge to round the pineapple, leaving the leaves raised (Photo 10). The tapered edge of this gouge allows you to reach into the corners between the leaves more easily. Define the shapes of the bottom leaves the same way you did for the top ones, beveling them so they appear to overlap.

If you like, you can now undercut the leaves slightly with a knife (Photo 12). Don't get carried away or you'll make the leaf tips too narrow and pointed. Remember, they are cross-grain, and will be fragile. A carving like this one, which may be displayed outdoors, needs to be sturdy to stand up to the elements. Remove a little wood to make the carving appear less "blocky," but not so much as to weaken it.

Carved pineapples were often painted gold. In some cases they were actually gilded with thin sheets of real gold. But this is an expensive and tricky process, so I used gold colored enamel paint instead. I selected enamel paints because I plan to display this carving outdoors. Enamels are more weather-resistant than other paints and were preferred by seafarers.

Pineapple

Photo 13

To display the pineapple, drill a small hole in the back and hang it up on a nail. This carving adds charm indoors or out. If you hang it on your front door, the natural effects of weathering will help to enhance the antique look.

So, try carving one for your home. The sight of a cheerful pineapple on the door will warm the hearts of visitors on even the coldest winter days. ■

Color the leaves green, again using an enamel paint (Photo 13). Use a no. 8 flat synthetic sable brush for the large areas, and a no. 4 pointed one for the edges of the leaves. Let the paint dry thoroughly.

You can leave your pineapple like this, but if you want it to look more antique, here's a technique to speed up the aging process. First, spray a light coat of lacquer, like Deft Clear Wood Finish, on the carving. This will seal the wood and keep too much paint from rubbing off during the steps that follow.

Next, sand the pineapple very lightly with 220-grit garnet paper. This removes a bit of paint from the high spots to duplicate the effects of weathering.

Photo 14

Then, brush on a coat of Wood Finish by Minwax in Special Walnut. Wipe it off promptly (Photo 14). The stain will remain in the crevices of the carving and darken them. It will also tone down the brightness of the paint, making it look more aged and mellow. The undercoat of lacquer keeps the stain from penetrating too deeply into the wood and darkening it too much. It also keeps the mineral spirits in the stain from softening and removing the enamel paint.

Thoroughbred Horse

Color Photo Page 47

Thoroughbred Horse

Today, it's hard to believe just how important the horse was to our grandparents. Horses provided the power to clear forests and plow fields. In many rural communities they were the only means of transportation until well into this century.

Now, however, the working horse is largely a thing of the past. In modern, industrialized countries, horses are kept mainly for pleasure, riding, showing, and of course, racing.

The Thoroughbred race horse is built for speed over short distances. It is lightweight but strong, with well-defined muscle structure. When carved into wood this well-defined muscle structure makes for interesting surface textures, which are important in relief carvings because they help the subject to stand out.

This carving is done in low relief. It creates the illusion of depth by the use of perspective rather than by cutting deeply into the wood to round the shapes. Relief carvings of this type require careful planning to make all the elements work well together. This project will help you to understand how the different elements, such as the foreground, subject, background, and horizon relate to each other.

Photo 2

It isn't necessary to take the entire background down a perfectly uniform ⅛ in. Just bevel it down to the outline cuts you made around the horse and barn. Texture the sky with a series of shallow tool cuts. You'll notice that removing the background pares away some of the lines of the pattern. You'll redraw these lines later.

If you feel your tool starting to dig in and raise splinters, you're carving against the grain. Turn the board around and carve from the opposite direction. Go slowly and don't try to remove too much at one time. Be especially careful around the delicate legs. A slip here could gouge out an important part of the carving.

Photo 1

Trace the design onto a piece of pine or basswood measuring ¾ in. thick by 7¾ in. wide by 10 in. long. Then outline the horse and barn with a 6 mm V-gouge (Photo 1). As this is a low relief carving, you don't need to cut down any deeper than ⅛ in. Don't make a V-gouge cut across the bottom of the horse's hooves or the lower edge of the barn. These will be blended with the foreground later.

After the outlining is finished, use a fairly large gouge of medium sweep, like a 20 mm no. 5, to remove the background (Photo 2). I'm using a fishtail gouge because the shape makes it easier to get into some of the tight spots to remove the wood. Leave the foreground raised; it will be textured later. Also, don't cut in close around the ears at this point.

Photo 3

To remove the background around the ears, hold the gouge in the pencil grip and use the corner to whittle away the wood (Photo 3). To clean out the wood between the front legs, you could use a small V-gouge. However, you can remove the wood more cleanly in this narrow section with the method of setting-in, as we did with the Pineapple carving.

Thoroughbred Horse

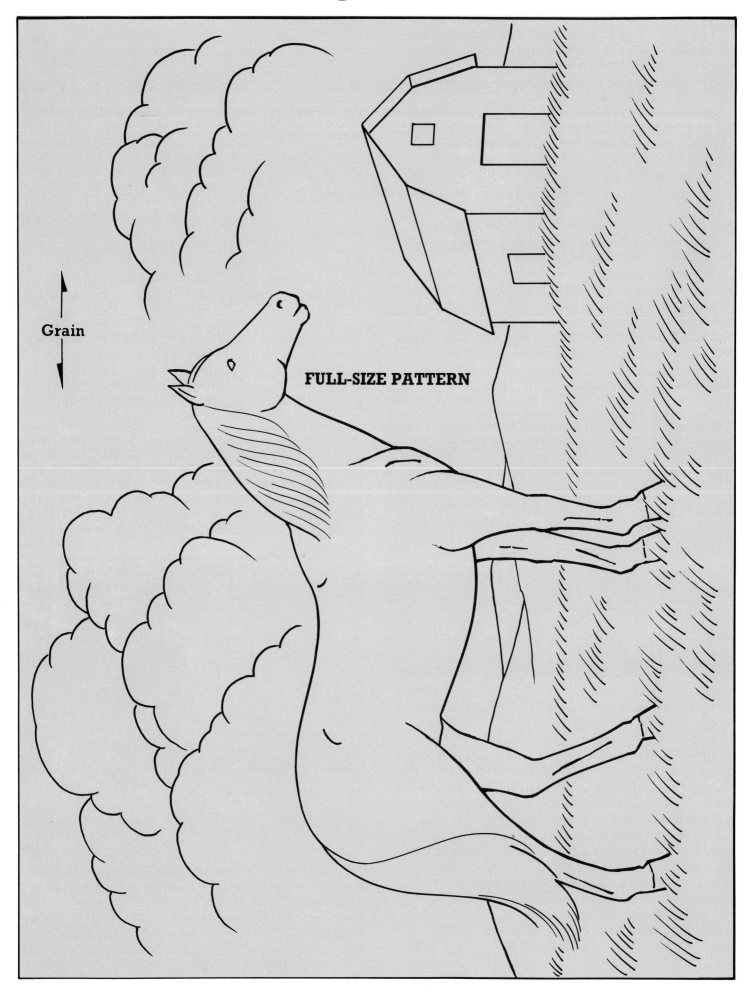

Grain

FULL-SIZE PATTERN

Thoroughbred Horse

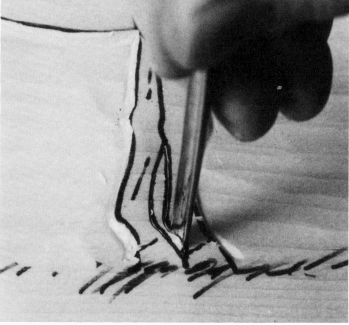

Photo 4

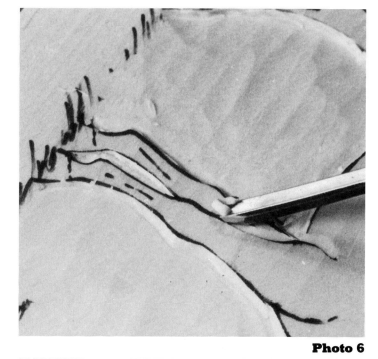

Photo 6

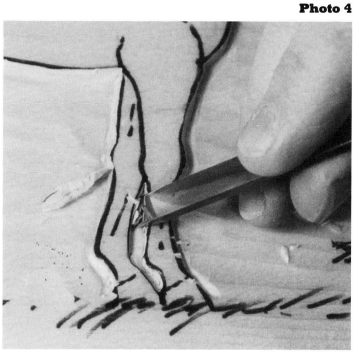

Photo 5

Photo 7

Now make vertical cuts down along the lines you have drawn, using gouges that have sweeps matching the curve of the line. I used an 8 mm no. 2 and 4 mm no. 8 for this (Photo 4). Then carefully scoop the wood out with the same gouges (Photo 5).

Next use the V-gouge to cut along the line that separates the two front legs (Photo 6). Do the same with the hind legs. Pare down the wood with the 8 mm no. 2 gouge so that it looks as though one leg is in front of the other (Photo 7).

Thoroughbred Horse

Photo 8

Round the sharp edges of the horse using the 8 mm no. 2 again (Photo 8). Make sure your tools are sharp so the cuts will be clean and smooth, and always work with the grain. On some of the horse's rounded contours you may have to carve part of the curve in one direction and then switch and finish the curve by carving from the opposite direction. Just watch grain direction carefully, and be ready to switch if the tool starts to dig in.

Photo 9

Now you can begin detailing the horse. Start by texturing the mane and tail. I'm using a 3 mm V-gouge to make the fine lines (Photo 9). Use the same tool to "draw in" the eye, mouth and nostril.

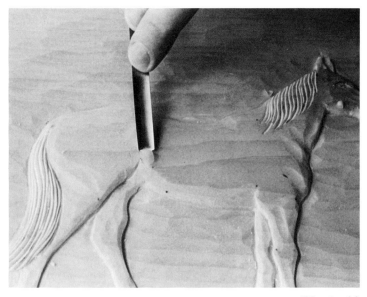

Photo 10

If you like, you can now contour some of the major muscle groups on the horse. Good reference photos or anatomy drawings can be very helpful here. Hollow out the shapes with an 8 mm no. 5 gouge (Photo 10).

Photo 11

Once the horse is finished, you can move on to the barn. Use a 3 mm V-gouge to outline the roof. Then bevel down the side of the barn with a 16 mm no. 2 gouge. Lower the front of the barn slightly with the same tool, leaving the roof raised above it. Outline the barn doors and window with the V-gouge (Photo 11). If you like, you can hollow them out with an 8 mm no. 5 gouge to create an illusion of depth.

Thoroughbred Horse

Photo 12

To carve the background, first redraw the lines with a pencil. Then, outline them with a V-gouge. Finally, bevel down the sky above the horizon, leaving the mountains raised (Photo 12).

Photo 14

A few clouds will add depth and interest to the sky. Lightly sketch them in with a pencil. To form the clouds, shape their upper edges with a 6 mm no. 11 gouge, called a veiner (Photo 14). Use the veiner instead of a V-gouge, because its rounded bottom leaves a softer edge. This is more appropriate for cloud texture.

For a final touch, lightly sand any rough spots with 220-grit sandpaper. Don't oversand and remove the tool marks.

Photo 13

To detail the foreground, lightly texture the wood with tool marks. I used a 20 mm no. 5 gouge. Try to arrange the tool marks in a pleasing pattern. Then, add a few sprigs of grass around the horse's hooves with the 3 mm V-gouge (Photo 13).

Photo 15

A light coat of stain will help bring out the texture in your carving, and increase the feeling of depth. With a flat panel like this it is a good idea to finish the sides and back the same way you do the front. This will insure that both sides of the wood are affected equally by humidity changes, and helps prevent warping. I used Wood Finish by Minwax in Special Walnut (Photo 15).

The horse is a fun project, and you'll find that you can use the same basic techniques to make a relief carving from just about any horse or animal drawing. This carving looks good hung on a wall like a picture. You could even make a barn wood frame for it. It also makes a great gift for any horse enthusiast in your family. ■

Driftwood Troll

Color Photo Page 47

Driftwood Troll

This carving is of a wood spirit or troll. Those who lived in the mountainous regions of Europe traditionally believed that the forests — even the trees themselves — were inhabited by supernatural beings. They considered these spirits the protectors of the forest, trees and animals. This belief was so strong that when a tree was cut down, rituals were observed to appease the spirits within. Some customs were so persistent that even today people "knock-on-wood," an ancient superstition intended to prevent wood spirits from causing mischief.

This carving represents one of these spirits as an old man whose form has become part of the tree he inhabits. This style of carving has been popular for centuries in the rural mountain regions of Northern Europe, where people still feel a close kinship to nature.

It seems natural to carve a figure like this in a log or piece of driftwood rather than a smooth finished plank. The rough textures of the wood and bark become part of the carving itself. This troll is made from a piece of red cedar driftwood, 4 in. wide and 14 in. long, found on the shore of an Adirondack lake. In working with wood like this, you need to be flexible and adapt the design to the shape of each individual piece of wood.

Driftwood can be difficult to carve. The most interesting wood often comes from trees like cedar, with tough and stringy grain. Soaking in water, often for many years, the wood's natural oils and resins leach out, leaving it brittle and porous. So, you may find it splits and chips when you try to carve it.

However, don't worry about small pieces that break off unexpectedly. Just change your design a bit to accommodate the new shape of the wood. These small slips will give your troll a unique character.

You can lessen the danger of splitting by working slowly. Don't try to take out too much wood with any one cut. It also helps if your tools are extra sharp before you start. Check your tools periodically as you carve, and strop them as needed to maintain a really keen edge. Grit from a sandy shore often becomes embedded in the wood fibers and can dull your tools quickly.

Before you begin carving, flatten the back side of the driftwood by cutting a section off on the band saw. Then plane it smooth.

Driftwood that has soaked a long time may have a surface that's too rough and crumbly to carve well. Pare it down to a firm working surface with a large gouge like this 60 mm no. 6 (Photo 1). You shouldn't have to go down very deep, perhaps about ¼ in. Just clean off the weathered fibers until you get to solid wood.

Photo 1

Photo 2

Screw a hardwood holding block to the back of the driftwood just as you did with the Merganser Decoy project. Then, clamp the block in the vise to hold the driftwood while you work on it.

Next, draw your pattern on the wood. Don't worry about following my design exactly. Feel free to change the lines with some freehand drawing of your own to take advantage of the natural contours of your particular piece (Photo 2).

Driftwood Troll

FULL-SIZE PATTERN

Grain

Driftwood Troll

Outline the eyebrows with a 12 mm V-gouge. Use the same gouge to define the hairline (Photo 4). Then smooth the forehead down to the hairline with a 12 mm no. 5 gouge, leaving the eyebrows raised. With the same gouge, bevel the mustache area down to the nose notch (Photo 5). Now begin shaping the nose by outlining it with the 12 mm no. 10 gouge. Make this cut about ¼ in. deep (Photo 6).

Photo 3

The basic procedure for carving the face is similar in principle to the one used to carve the faces on Alvah Dunning and St. Nicklaus. First establish the profile by carving a notch ⅜ in. deep underneath the nose with a 12 mm no. 10 gouge, and another across the eye line (Photo 3). You will probably want to use a mallet to help tap the gouge through the wood.

Photo 5

Photo 6

Photo 7

Pare the cheeks with the 12 mm no. 5 gouge (Photo 7). Don't make the cheeks perfectly flat; round them

Photo 4

Driftwood Troll

Photo 8

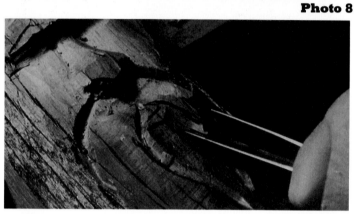

Photo 9

Photo 10

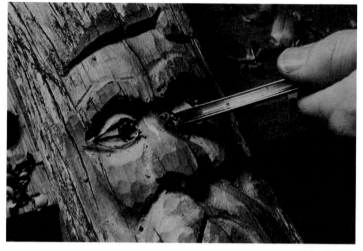

Photo 11

Now the major shapes of the face are roughed out, and you can begin the detailing. Start with the eyes, the feature that gives your troll a feeling of life and expression. Draw in the basic shape before you start. Then shape above and below the eyeball with a 6 mm no. 11 veiner to create a rounded surface (Photo 11). Next, use a 6 mm V-gouge to shape the upper and lower eyelids (Photo 12).

Photo 12

Photo 13

slightly so they follow the curved shape of the log. Now, while you have the 12 mm no. 5 gouge in hand, carve away some wood from the top of the nose, sloping it down to the eye notch (Photo 8). Round the sides of the nose slightly with the same tool.

Next, redraw the mustache and outline it with the 12 mm V-gouge (Photo 9). Make the ends of the mustache flow out into the rough portions of the wood with curved lines. This will help give your troll a wild, woodsy look.

Bevel the top ends of the mustache down to the nose and remove the wood between the two halves of the mustache with the 12 mm no. 5 gouge. Then take the 12 mm no. 10 gouge and shape the outline of the sides of the head down to the mustache (Photo 10). This cut defines the face and gives a more rounded look to the cheeks. It makes the troll look as though he is peering out from the tree.

To shape the pupil of the eye use a 7 mm no. 8 gouge (Photo 13). Clean the chips out of the corner of the eye

Driftwood Troll

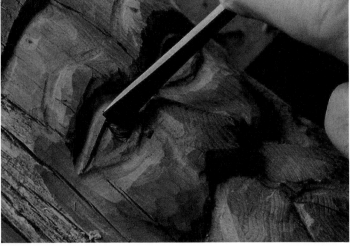

Photo 14

with the 12 mm no. 5 fishtail gouge (Photo 14). Hold it vertically and use the angled corner to make the cuts.

Photo 15

Carve the mouth by using the same techniques you just used for the eye pupil. I made his mouth open to suggest wind blowing through the tree branches. Shape the lower lip by cutting a groove ¼ in. below the open mouth with the 7 mm no. 8 gouge (Photo 15).

Photo 16

Photo 17

To give the hair a fluffy, dense appearance, first shape the major hair masses with the 12 mm V-gouge (Photo 16). Then texture the hair, beard, mustache, and eyebrows by carving long flowing cuts with a 6 mm V-gouge (Photo 17). Trail these out over the natural surface of the wood so your troll looks as though he is part of the tree.

Photo 18

For the final details, carve shallow wrinkles under his eyes and across his forehead with the 6 mm no. 8 gouge (Photo 18). The rounded cutting edge of the gouge will create a softer line than the sharply angled V-gouge.

Next use a small piece of 220-grit garnet paper to clean out any tiny wood splinters that might remain in the corners. But don't smooth away any of the tool marks. They give the troll's face a craggy texture that enhances his mysterious woodland character.

To show off the tool marks even further, finish the carved portion of the wood with paste wax. I used a no. 8 bristle paintbrush to spread a thin, even layer of wax over all of the carved details. Then I buffed it out with a clean shoe brush. This will bring out the rich colors found in driftwood, and give it a soft, mellow sheen that accentuates the carved features. Leave the rest of the wood unfinished. The contrast between the polished troll face and the remaining weathered driftwood creates an unusually striking effect.

To display your carving, drill a ⅛ in. diameter hole in the back, angled slightly upward. Then hang it on a small finishing nail.

This project is really fun because you have so much freedom in carving it. Don't be concerned with making any of the features exact. Just pick up an interesting piece of wood and use your imagination. ■

Tobacconist's Indian

Tobacconist's Indian

Trade signs date to antiquity. At a time when most of the population couldn't read, merchants found it good business to hang a symbol of their trade outside their shops. A tavern might display a large bunch of carved grapes, while a barber placed the familiar red and white striped pole by his door. But perhaps the most recognizable trade sign of all was the tobacconist's Indian.

These figures originated in England, where tobacco was considered a gift of the Indians and hailed as a cure for almost all diseases. By the 17th century, small Indian figures were being carved and set in front of tobacconists' shops all across England. The custom spread to the United States, where it was well-established by the 1860's.

At first, most wooden Indians were made by ship-carvers, who considered them a mere sideline. However, as the shipbuilding industry changed, and ornate figureheads were no longer fashionable, more and more carvers turned exclusively to trade figures.

Many different styles of wooden Indians were popular. This particular figure is modeled after the Indian princess which stood in front of the tobacconist's shop in my hometown, when I was a boy. I later discovered that the unknown carver who made it was undoubtedly influenced by the work of Samuel Robb. Robb, the best known carver of wooden Indians, made dozens of these figures in the late 1800's. This Indian carving is similar to one he made in 1881.

The Indian figure itself is 25 in. tall. It stands atop a 5 in. high pedestal, and both the Indian and pedestal are carved from a single block of wood. The pedestal raises the carving and provides it with a stable base. And the pedestal gives you a clamping area to hold the figure down as you work. A wooden Indian of this size would probably be displayed on a larger wooden base with advertisements painted on its sides.

While this type of carving could technically be called sculpture, the basic steps followed to shape the Indian and carve the details are the same as for relief carving.

I used white pine, the wood traditionally used to carve this figure. You'll need a block measuring 6 in. thick by 9 in. wide by 30 in. long. If you can't locate a block this size, simply laminate one from 2 in. thick wood.

There are a few difficulties inherent in working with a single large block. For one thing, you may not be able to find one that is knot-free. Don't worry, a few knots won't spoil the overall effect of the carving as long as they don't fall in an area that will be finely detailed, like the face.

A large block of wood is also more prone to splitting as you carve. Some splits can be prevented by working with well-seasoned wood. But a few are inevitable as you remove large amounts of wood from the block and release internal stresses. As long as splits do not actually threaten to break your carving in two, they only enhance the weathered look of a carving like this.

In the instructions for making this carving I have mentioned all the different tools I used. The sizes listed are only suggestions. There is a great deal of flexibility in what tools you can use. For instance, if you don't have some of the very large gouges, like the 60 mm no. 6, you can substitute a smaller one, like the 25 mm or 30 mm no. 5. It will just take you a little longer to remove the same amount of wood. So feel free to experiment with the tools you already have, before you add a lot of specialized gouges to your collection.

Photo 1

Enlarge the Indian pattern to full size and, using carbon paper, copy the front view onto the wood (Photo 1).

Tobacconist's Indian

Grain

1 SQUARE = 1 INCH

Tobacconist's Indian

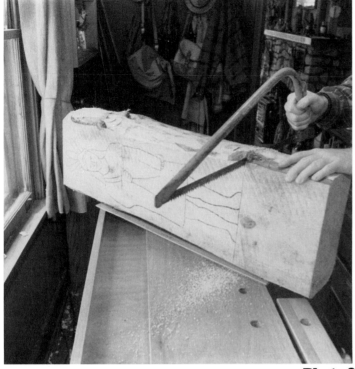

Turn the block on its side and make saw cuts along the top of the base, stopping at the foot (Photo 2). Make similar cuts along the bottom of the robe to the legs. These cuts act as guides when you remove the excess wood with a gouge. This step saves time in the roughing-out process. The top of the base and the bottom of the robe are about the only straight lines on this carving, and cutting them with a saw insures a more accurate shape.

Place the wood faceup on your bench, with a scrap board under it to protect your bench top. At this stage you don't need to fasten the block down, it's too heavy to go far.

Rough out the Indian by cutting down vertically across the grain with your largest gouge and heaviest mallet (Photo 3). I'm using a 50 mm no. 7 Swiss-style fishtail gouge and a 36 ounce lignum vitae mallet. Never use a metal hammer to strike the gouge. Metal has no give and it will split the end of your tool. Also, let the weight of the mallet provide the power. Don't try to muscle the gouge through the wood with arm power. Letting the mallet do the work will be easier on you and your tools.

Photo 4

As you come in closer to the outline of the Indian, you will need a smaller gouge to get into some of the sharp angles, especially around the head. I used a 25 mm no. 11 gouge (Photo 4). Don't round the Indian yet, it will be easier to keep track of where you are in the carving if you establish the outline first.

Photo 3

Photo 5

When the front view is roughed out, turn the blank on its side and sketch in the side view (Photo 5).

Tobacconist's Indian

Photo 6

Photo 7

Now that you have taken off a fair amount of wood, the carving is considerably lighter and must be fastened down before you continue. I used a large pipe clamp to secure the piece for the remaining carving steps.

With the Indian clamped faceup on the bench, use your handsaw to make cuts on the front along the bottom edge of the robe and the top edge of the base, stopping at the legs. These are similar to the cuts you made earlier from the side. Reclamp the carving facedown, and repeat the saw cuts along the robe and base on the back. These cuts serve as a guide and keep you from accidentally removing too much wood in the leg area.

Now, you are ready to start shaping the profile. Use a large gouge like a 60 mm no. 6 Swiss fishtail to remove the wood. This gouge is flatter than the 50 mm no. 7 and doesn't bite as deeply into the wood. The cuts it makes are a bit smoother.

Rough out the back first. On the finished carving it is flatter and less detailed than the front. That way, when you turn the carving over and begin roughing out the front, you won't have to worry about damaging any of the more delicate areas like the face (Photo 6). Leave plenty of wood in the leg area. The legs are the most fragile part of the carving and will be shaped later.

When the major outlines are roughed out, the next step is to begin blocking out the arms. Set in the left arm by cutting down vertically along the outline with the 60 mm no. 6 gouge. In the narrow area between the tobacco box and the upper arm I used a 16 mm V-gouge. When using these big tools on a softwood like pine, don't cut directly on the outlines you have drawn. Stay about ¼ in. away from them. The force needed to drive the tools through the wood can cause the fibers to crush slightly and splinter. Later, as you carve down to the outline with smaller gouges, this damaged wood will be removed.

Set in the arm in stages. First cut down vertically about ½ in. using the 60 mm no. 6 gouge. Then, using the same tool, scoop out the wood surrounding the arm to the depth of the cut. Repeat this process until you have gone down about 1½ in. (Photo 7). Trying to remove all the wood in one step would exert too much pressure on the wood and cause it to split.

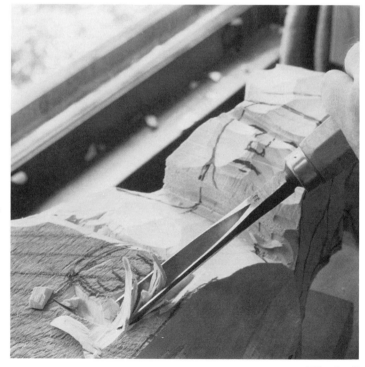

Photo 8

Turn the blank onto its back to work on the right arm. With the 16 mm V-gouge outline the arm about ½ in. deep (Photo 8). Then use the 60 mm no. 6 gouge to bevel the excess wood, leaving the arm raised (Photo 9).

Tobacconist's Indian

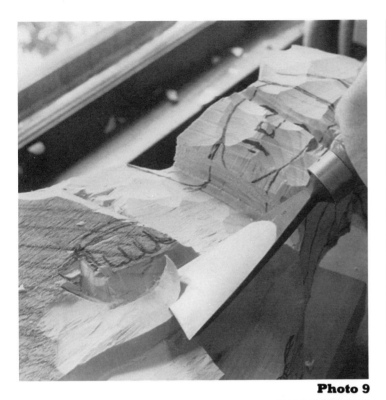

Photo 9

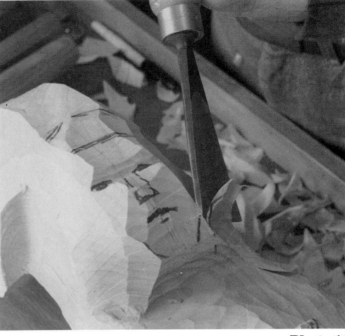

Photo 11

After rounding the body, take off the sharp angles on the head. You can rough out the feathers quickly with a large gouge like the 60 mm no. 6. Use the same tool to round the sides of the face (Photo 11). But work more slowly here; you don't want to take off too much wood.

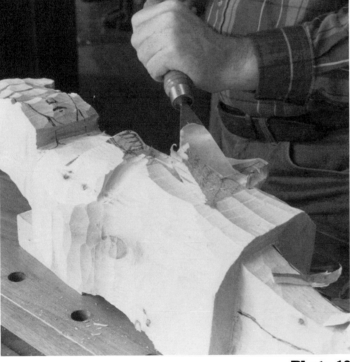

Photo 10

Now, the major levels have been established, just as you would do with a relief carving. The next step is to begin rounding the corners with the 60 mm gouge (Photo 10). In some areas, like the right arm, you may find it helpful to go to a smaller gouge like a 30 mm to avoid removing too much wood. As you progress to finer and finer details on the Indian you will find yourself using smaller gouges. They take out less wood, and allow you more control.

Photo 12

When the entire carving is rounded to your satisfaction, you can begin carving the face. First, draw in the headband and pare away the wood above and below that. Next, draw in the lines for the hair. The basic steps followed to carve the face are the same as for the Driftwood Troll project, but the features are smaller and more delicate.

Outline the hairline with the large V-gouge (Photo 12).

Tobacconist's Indian

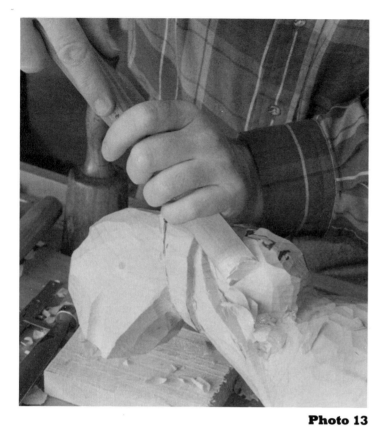

Photo 13

Then thin the sides of the face with a 30 mm no. 2 (Photo 13). Also thin the neck with the same tools.

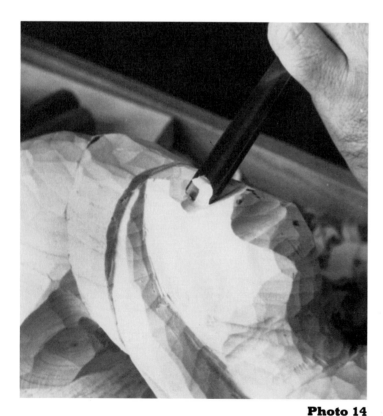

Photo 14

Cut a notch across the face at the eyeline with a 12 mm no. 10 gouge. Make another notch across the bottom of the nose (Photo 14). Outline the nose with a 7 mm no. 8 gouge (Photo 15). Then smooth and round the cheeks with a small gouge like a 6 mm no. 2.

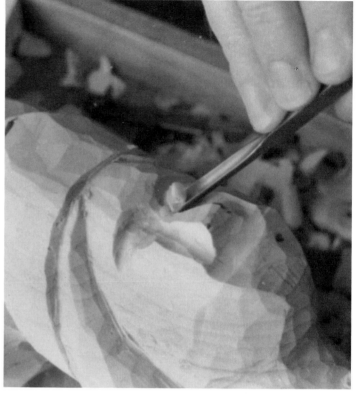

Photo 15

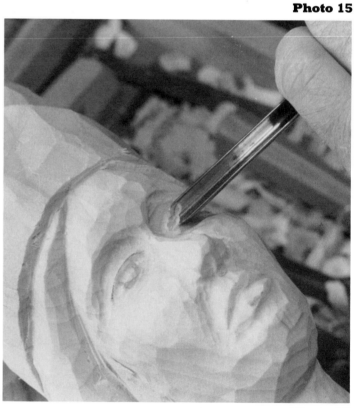

Photo 16

Carve the major shapes of the eye the same way you did on the Driftwood Troll. Shape above and below the eyeball with a 6 mm no. 11 veiner to create a rounded surface for the eye. Pencil in the upper eyelid and incise a shallow line along it with the small veiner (Photo 16). The rest of the details of the eyes can be applied later with paint, or you can carve the pupil with a small no. 8 gouge.

Tobacconist's Indian

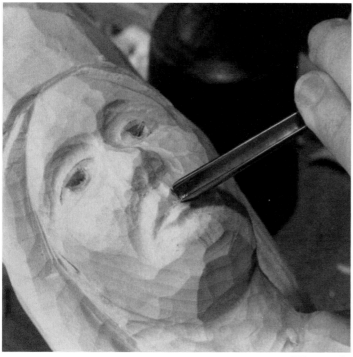

Photo 17

Photo 18

Bevel the thick edges of the feathers down from the back with the 30 mm no. 2 gouge. Don't make the feather edges too thin and delicate. Trade figures, like this Indian, were made to be solid and sturdy. They had to resist the effects of years of standing in front of a store exposed to the elements and the curious hands of passersby.

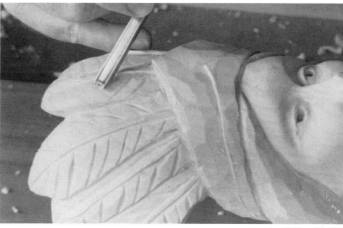

Photo 19

Carve the mouth next. Rough in the general shapes of the mouth with the veiner. Remember, the mouth is not a straight line; it has a gentle curve like a flattened "M." Shape the inside curve with a 6 mm V-gouge (Photo 17).

When carving a human figure, I like to carve the face before the other details. It gives me a better feeling for the personality of the person I'm carving and seems to make the rest of the work go more quickly.

To detail the feathers, first use a macaroni tool to carve two lines down the center of each feather, creating the central shaft. Then, cut in a few feather barb lines with the 6 mm V-gouge (Photo 19).

Next, shape the box, outlining it with a 12 mm V-gouge between the arm and the box. Then use the 30 mm no. 2 to shape the edges of the box. With the same tool, round the general shape of the arm. Cut a notch around the arm with the 12 mm no. 10 to form the arm band. Then, bevel the wood above and below the arm band with a 12 mm V-gouge.

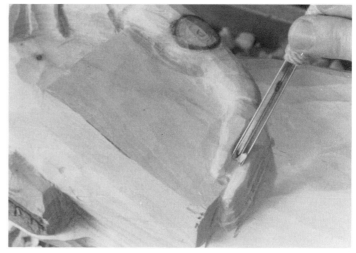

Photo 20

After the arm is rounded, use the 30 mm no. 2 gouge to block in the major planes of the hand. Hands can be tricky, so take a good look at your own in the same position before you begin carving. Carve the cuff of the sleeve with the 6 mm no. 11 veiner and use the same tool to define the individual fingers (Photo 20). Round the tips of the fingers with a small flat gouge.

Smooth off the front of the headdress with the 30 mm no. 2 gouge. Then hollow the back with a 24 mm no. 11. Use a 25 mm no. 5 fishtail gouge to smooth down the tool cuts (Photo 18). Then use a coping saw to cut out the excess wood between the individual feathers.

Tobacconist's Indian

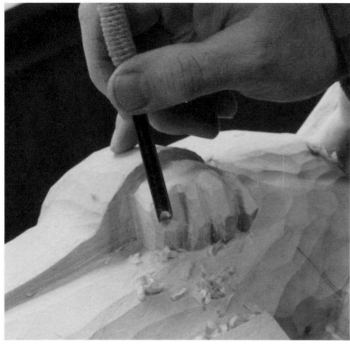

Photo 21

Turn the Indian onto its back and sketch in the robes. Then use the 12 mm V-gouge to outline where the robe drapes over the hand and down to the hem. Pare away the excess so the robe appears to overlap the hand and drape over the skirt.

Then, use the 25 mm no. 5 fishtail to block out the fist. Use the 6 mm veiner again to carve the fingers (Photo 21).

Photo 23

To model the folds of the skirt, make cuts tapering up from the hem toward the waist with a large gouge like a 24 mm no. 11 (Photo 23). Use a large gouge so the folds appear to fall gently, suggesting soft cloth. Put similar folds at the crook of the elbow and the back of the robe. Use a 6 mm V-gouge to incise a line along the hem of the skirt and the edges of the robe to form a border. If you like, you can texture the border of the skirt with small V-gouge cuts.

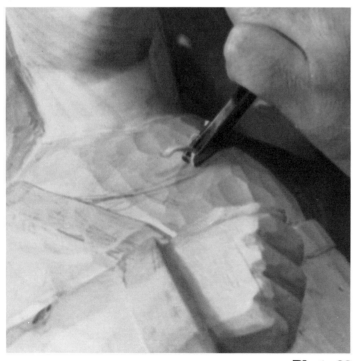

Photo 22

Outline the rest of the robe with the 12 mm V-gouge and pare away the excess wood with the fishtail. Carve the neckline of the shirt and the collar the same way (Photo 22).

Photo 24

The final step before shaping the legs is to detail the hair. Use the 6 mm V-gouge to incise lines to give the feeling of flowing strands of hair (Photo 24).

Up to this point the legs have been left blocky, to provide support for the body while it was being carved. If they had been carved to their final thin shapes earlier, they might have broken when the body was being roughed out.

Tobacconist's Indian

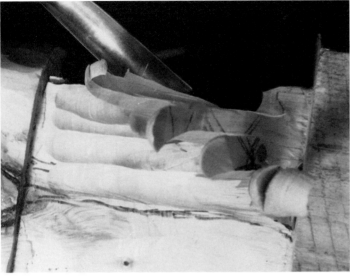

Photo 25

Photo 26

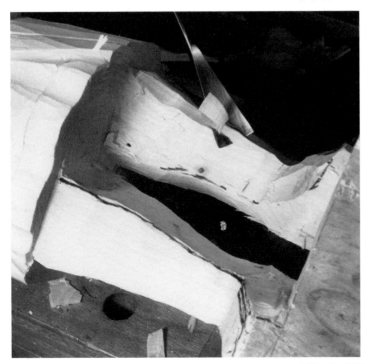

Photo 27

Photo 28

Start by removing the waste wood around the legs with the 24 mm veiner (Photo 25). Finish removing the waste wood by cutting down vertically along the contours of the legs with the 50 mm no. 7 gouge (Photo 26). Leave the legs square at this time, just as we did when roughing out the body, to help get the correct proportions. Then round the legs with the 25 mm no. 5 fishtail (Photo 27).

Once the legs are shaped, sketch in the moccasins. Outline the cuff with a 6 mm V-gouge (Photo 28). Then texture the fringe with the same tool.

Next, sand the face, hands, and legs with 120-grit paper, followed by 220-grit. The skin areas should be quite smooth. Sand the rest of the carving lightly to smooth off any rough edges, but don't remove all the tool marks.

Tobacconist's Indians were usually painted in bright, cheerful colors. I'm using oil paints thinned with turpentine to give this carving a softer, slightly aged look.

Tint the skin with a thin wash of burnt sienna. Paint the robes and headdress with your personal choice of colors. I used cadmium red medium, cerulean blue, and veridian green. The border on the robe is traditionally gold. The moccasins, box, and pedestal are burnt umber. After the paint has dried, you can tone the colors down further with a thin wash of burnt umber.

A complex project like this is quite a challenge. But the experience gained broadens your carving skills. Later on you'll discover that the things you've learned can also be applied to other carvings. ∎